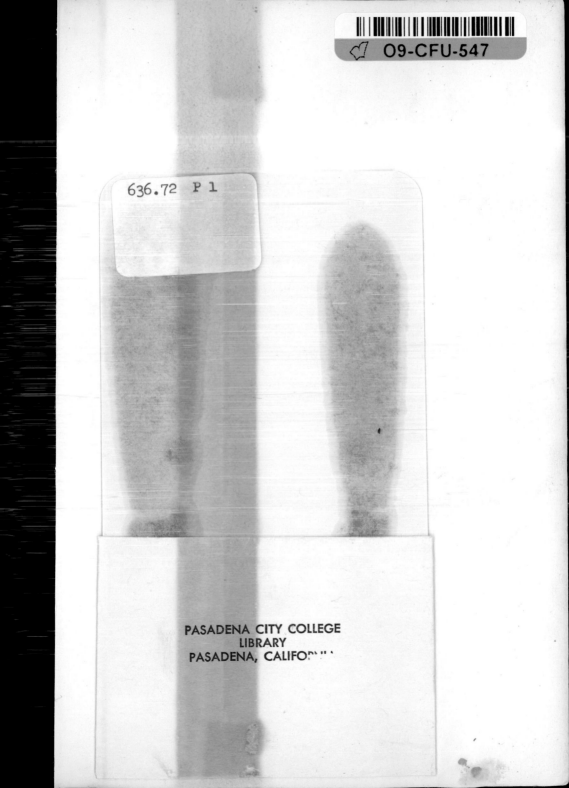

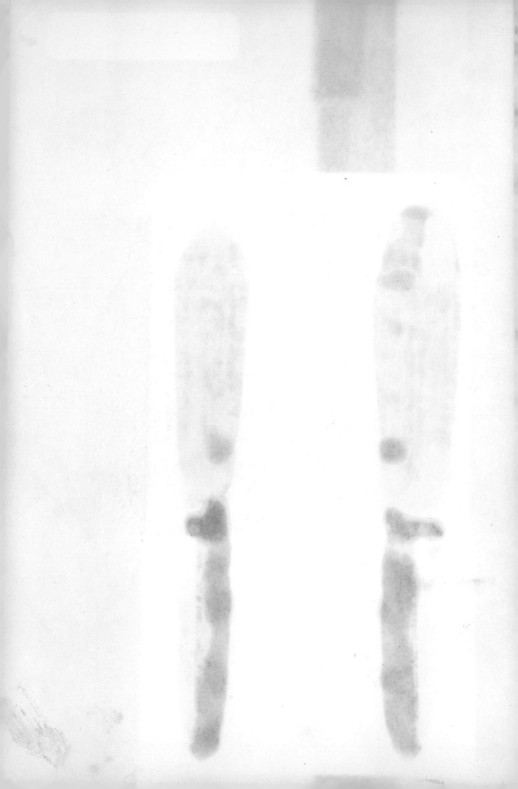

____LOVE
in the Lead

Other books by
Peter Brock Putnam

PETER, THE REVOLUTIONARY
TSAR

THE TRIUMPH OF THE
SEEING EYE

CAST OFF THE DARKNESS

"KEEP YOUR HEAD UP,
MR. PUTNAM!"

SEVEN BRITONS IN IMPERIAL
RUSSIA, 1698–1812

LOVE
in the Lead

The Fifty-Year Miracle of the Seeing Eye Dog

PETER BROCK PUTNAM

 A Sunrise Book • E. P. DUTTON • New York

For information contact: E.P. Dutton, 2 Park Avenue,
New York, N.Y. 10016

Library of Congress Cataloging in Publication Data:
Putnam, Peter.   Love in the lead.
   "A Sunrise book."   1. The Seeing Eye, inc., Morristown, N. J.—History.
2. Guide dogs—Training.   I. Title.   HV1780.S4P86   636.7'08'86   79-232

ISBN: 0-87690-309-X   ~~Pe. 636.72~~

Published simultaneously in Canada by Clarke, Irwin & Company
Limited, Toronto and Vancouver

Designed by Barbara Huntley

10 9 8 7 6 5 4 3 2 1

First Edition

Behind the human personalities of The Seeing Eye, there are dogs, and behind both dogs and humans are another group of humans: the instructors of The Seeing Eye. They are tough and tender, sensible and sensitive, hardheaded, good-humored, and great-hearted. They have steel nerves, iron constitutions, and hair-trigger reflexes. They give of themselves cheerfully and without stint. Indeed, they are very like their dogs.

I know of no class of human beings that I admire more. With affection and respect, this book is dedicated to the men and women instructors of The Seeing Eye, past, present, and future.

Contents

Eight pages of illustrations follow page 128

Preface

THIS IS the story of The Seeing Eye, the first school for the education of guide dogs * and blind humans in the United States. Its development was a uniquely cooperative venture, depending on the right combination of human ingredients at every stage in the process. As Morris Frank, one of its founders, insists, "If you know anything at all about the history of The Seeing Eye, you have to believe in the Good Lord—even if you're a damned atheist!"

Hyperbole is Morris's style, but I am tempted to agree with him here. Especially in its early days, the evolution of The Seeing Eye depended on such an extraordinary assortment of personalities and took so many unexpected twists and turns that serendipity is too pale a concept to explain it. It may be simpler, saner, and safer to account for it by a divinity forever stepping in with the right person or circumstance at the right time.

* Guide dog is the natural generic term for a dog that performs as a guide for a blind person, but when a school in California took the name Guide Dogs for the Blind, there was the danger that "guide dog" might indicate only a dog graduated from that school. As a result, The Seeing Eye, Leader Dogs for the Blind, and Guide Dogs for the Blind agreed among themselves to use "dog guide" as the generic term. To this writer, it seems almost as unnatural as dog police or dog shepherd. With apologies to the schools, therefore, and for the greater comfort of the reader, I have chosen to use guide dog.

Besides the main actors, there were many other characters who played significant and even crucial roles for longer or shorter periods, and I have known most of them, though some only glancingly. I have received much help from a number of them in writing this book and I am very much indebted to Stuart Grout, the executive vice president of The Seeing Eye, for giving me access to the school's files and for refusing to exert even the hint of censorship. Significant assistance of different kinds has come from all of the following: Jean Bernat, C. Warren Bledsoe, Adelaide Clifford Byers, G. William Debetaz, Edith Doudge De Heller, Morris and Lois Frank, Alfreda Galt, George Humphrey, Elizabeth Hutchinson, Marian Jobson, Joan Jones, Margaret Kibbee, Edward Myrose, Roger Taylor, George Werntz, Jr., Robert Whitstock, and Walter Abbott Wood III. Their universal eagerness to be helpful is a tribute to the school.

I have concentrated heavily on the early history, because the early years were the formative years. They witnessed the development of the methods, the goals, and the philosophy that guided the later period. Besides, Cinderella becomes less interesting after she marries the prince.

Since 1941, I have experienced the extraordinary partnership between dog and human that is at the heart of The Seeing Eye, and I think I understand in my bones the leadership role that the dogs played in the formation of Seeing Eye philosophy. For the dogs were leaders in more than the literal sense, and what gave the human leaders their direction was their ability to read the dogs' language.

I want to thank my wonderful typists, Beatrice Bilton, Mary Olivier, and Bunny Patee. Finally, I owe a tremendous debt to two people who spent many hundreds of hours poring over letters, clippings, articles, pamphlets, reports, and books. Both threw themselves into dull and painstaking research. Both made valuable suggestions for improving the style and structure of this book. They are my friend and reader, Peggy Waldron, and my very good friend and wife, Durinda Dobbins Putnam.

Introduction: Partnership

"Is SHE really any good to you?" The question came from a veterinary doctor, and the "she" was Minnie, my first Seeing Eye dog whom he had just returned to me at my Princeton dormitory room. A week before, prior to a critical surgical operation, she had been on the verge of death, but, except for the taped bandage which circled her middle, there was no sign of it now. In her joy at coming home, she wriggled into my lap, licked my face, and nipped my hands. Then she made a circular dash around the room, slipped on a throw rug, scrambled to her feet, sneezed, and, to cover her embarrassment at my laughter, began to chew on one arm of the sofa.

It was an exhibition of thoroughly random behavior, and it is no wonder that there was a note of genuine skepticism beneath the doctor's smiling question.

"Is she really any good to you?"

I cannot recall my reply. Even to me, the transformation of Minnie, the irresponsible schoolgirl, into Minerva, the trustworthy guide, was always a miracle. Miracles are better demonstrated than described, and my best answer would have been to pick up her harness. She always dove into it eagerly, without waiting for me to slip it over her head, and, instantly, she became a new person, serious, self-possessed, and intent on her work.

Outside, she would tug me across the campus at four miles an hour, ignoring the tempting squirrels that scampered across the grass but dutifully mindful of the many steps along the walk, threading her way carefully through the moving crowd of students but impatiently nudging aside the slower walkers by nosing them in the calves, hurrying across streets that were deserted but stopping short in the face of oncoming traffic. All these things she would do, and yet they would have provided only a partial answer to the doctor's question.

The relationship between a Seeing Eye dog and its master is as complex as that of a child and its parents. Indeed, acquiring a dog is not unlike adopting a child. The weeks each applicant must spend at The Seeing Eye's school in Morristown, New Jersey, are a kind of character examination, and graduation, like the certificate of adoption, is not the end but the beginning of a long emotional adjustment. There are many irritations, as well as gratifications, but in the end the successful dog and master arrive at a working partnership whose balance is equaled in few human families.

Even during my first days at the school, I discovered that, while my adopted child was already perfectly educated in the partnership, I still had everything to learn. Minerva did her part faithfully, but I often failed to understand the signals which came up through the harness handle. Unprepared for her sudden, precise stops, I might slip over curbs or stumble up steps, and, more often than I care to think, my awkwardness in following her turns cost her a bruised paw.

However, basic coordination was much easier to master than orientation. It was Minnie's duty to guide me around obstacles as we walked, but it was I who must direct her, by word and gesture, along the route I wished to travel. In total darkness, I had to know where I was, where I was going, and how to get there in a series of lefts, rights, or forwards.

Perhaps I was unusually backward, but I found this a tremendous strain. Sweating with concentration, I would suddenly go blank as to the number of blocks to the next turn, and fall instant prey to all the nameless anxieties of a lost child. Even back at Princeton, whose terrain ought to have been so familiar from the sighted years, I often misjudged distances or angles on the diagonally intersecting walks, steps, and archways of the campus.

My uncertainty was fully as nerve-racking for Minerva as for myself, but each problem had its resolution. To illustrate both, I can find no better anecdote than one from the life of my second dog, Wick.

We were walking down a country road one evening when a recent acquaintance, pulling up in his car, asked me to stop by for a drink. I agreed, but suggested that I continue on foot for the exercise. The road was new to me and without curbs and sidewalks to act as landmarks, but I knew his house to be some distance ahead on the left-hand side, and I assumed that he would hail me as I came up.

Five hundred yards farther on, I discarded this assumption, but there was no one to ask. I turned back. Up and down that road we went, trying tentative rights and lefts, and the more impatient my gestures became, the more uncertain and hesitant Wick grew.

Nearly an hour later, having passed it fully a dozen times, we turned into the proper driveway, and I made it all up to a much relieved Wick with a shower of pats and praises, but the climax was yet to come. Over a month later, when for the first time we passed that way again, Wick, remembering the anxieties of that afternoon, paused before the elusive driveway, as if to inquire whether I wanted to go in, and in all the years since then he has never failed to hesitate at that same spot.

It was less my impatience while lost than the pats and "atta good boys" which followed that had impressed the driveway on Wick's memory. This sort of reward is the motivating mainspring of every Seeing Eye dog. His pleasure in his master's praise seems sufficient compensation for every hardship. An aggressive terrier whom we were forced to pass almost daily used to persecute Wick with menacing sorties on our flanks for nearly a hundred yards, all the while screaming canine insults in a high staccato bark. I managed to congratulate Wick so warmly after each running of the gauntlet that he seemed almost to look forward to the ordeal, only quickening his pace a little to have it behind him. Then, he would jump up on me joyously, saying plainer than any words could tell: "Oh, what a good boy am I!"

And so, through a thousand little episodes and adjustments, the child and the parent become full partners. The rigid mechanics of command and obey dissolve into a co-operation as instinctive and a coordination as spontaneous as waltzing. I vividly recall the thrill of a moment when Wick and I were walking home from the post office one afternoon. As we passed a grocery store where I often stopped, Wick hesitated.

For one split second, we were suspended on the doubt of Wick's implied question. At the slightest sign from me, we could have turned in perfect unison into the store. Upon my negative "huh-huh," we resumed the steady flow of our direction without breaking stride. The communication had been perfectly clear, and yet the whole movement was so smooth that I believe neither Wick's question nor my answer could have been detected by any but a trained observer.

Such harmony of motion is a consequence of long practice, but it is derived from a deeper level of communion. The most valuable lesson a Seeing Eye dog owner can learn is also the simplest. He must understand that he is blind and that his dog can see. This adds up to a human limitation and a canine potentiality. On the other hand, he has the power of reason, while his dog has certain powerfully irrational instincts, and this adds up to a human potentiality and a canine limitation.

Both have the power to love, which can alone make possible the patience, the concentration, and the self-discipline necessary to weld the two—the man-animal and the dog-animal—into a corporate unit. Through love, they learn to recognize and to forgive both their own and each other's limitations and, therefore, to realize their joint potentialities.

The discovery of this concept of joint self-realization opened a new world for me. Before blindness, having recognized the existence of no limitations, my life was confined to potentialities. Seven months after blindness, the acquisition of Minnie helped me realize that the only way to overcome a limitation is to understand and accept it.

Together, Minnie and I could do anything, and I felt a greater confidence and appetite for life than I had ever known. Returning to Princeton, I found that my academic activities could not fully satisfy this appetite. In response to a secret yearning, I took piano lessons for the first time. To work off steam, I swam seventy to a hundred laps daily in the gym pool. Fulfilling a freshman dream, I ran for and was elected to the presidency of the Princeton Triangle Club, whose musical comedy I helped to write and direct. Dwarfing everything else, I met and fell in love with the girl I was to marry, Durinda.

Minnie was with me through all of it, in the lecture halls and classrooms, in the piano studios, beside the pool, on the stage of the theater, and on the floor of the train swaying off to New York or Northampton for weekends with Durinda. All these things demanded varying degrees of sacrifice from the undeviating Minnie. I could demand it from Minnie then, as I could demand it from Wick later, not because I regarded either of them as a tool, but because I did not.

Any attempt to define a Seeing Eye dog as a tool, a guiding instrument for a blind man, breaks down upon the love which alone enables that instrument to function. This love can no more make the dog the tool of the master than it can make the master the tool of the dog. It forges a bond of sympathy so strong that their happiness becomes interdependent.

It is so with my dog today, but it was from Minnie, my first dog, that I learned it first. My very love for her compelled me to force my will upon her in the knowledge that my every success would be her justification, that my every failure would imply her betrayal, and that my happiness would include her own.

Men find this same dynamic inspiration in the love of their own kind, but there is a sense in which a dog strikes closer to the heart, because a dog seems to understand organically, without benefit of reasoned explanation. Minnie could have no understanding of the sounds of the piano, of the words of the lectures, or of the splashings in the pool, and yet she seemed able to understand better than anyone their deeper meaning for my—and therefore her—happiness. And, to answer the doctor's question at last, it was in this compelling love and understanding that I realized the full and true measure of Minnie's good to me.

BOOK I

Birth by Accident

CHAPTER 1

Fortunate
Fields

THE SEEING EYE's official birthday is January 29, 1929, but its roots go back much further. We could trace them all the way back to the moment in prehistory some twenty thousand years ago when human beings first domesticated the ancestor of the dog. For our purposes here, we may propose the day in 1914 when Dorothy Harrison Wood returned from Europe with a German shepherd dog named Hans von Saarbrücken. That event combined three necessary conditions for the evolution of The Seeing Eye. First, Hans was a shepherd. Second, he was an extraordinary specimen of the breed. Finally, his mistress was a remarkable woman.

Dorothy Leib Harrison was born on May 30, 1886, into an old Philadelphia family. Her father, Charles Custis Harrison, a onetime provost of the University of Pennsylvania, owned a prosperous suger-refining company. Dorothy was the youngest of six children, with three brothers and two sisters. Educated at the Agnes Irwin School in Philadelphia and the Rathgowrie School in Eastbourne, England, she was raised as a blue blood who became, as matter of course, a member of the Daughters of the American Revolution, the Colonial Dames of America, the Descendants of the Signers of the Declaration of Independence, and the Society of

Magna Carta Dames. In 1906, at the age of twenty, she was married to Walter Abbott Wood, Jr.

Walter Wood was considerably older than Dorothy. A New York State senator, he owned a mowing and reaping machine company in Hoosick Falls. Living on his comfortable estate, they had two sons, Walter III, in 1907 and Harrison in 1914. Dorothy interested herself in an agricultural experiment in the selective breeding of cattle to increase milk productivity. She was an aristocrat imbued with the work ethic. She was also extremely observant, and from the time she acquired her dog Hans, her keen eyes and mind observed him.

As a German shepherd, Hans belonged to a breed that had been herding sheep in Central Europe for two centuries. Throughout history, the vast majority of dogs have been workers. They have been used to hunt, track, or retrieve game, to haul carts or sleds, to guard homes or farms, to rescue lost travelers or trail fugitives, to dig truffles, to kill rats, or to herd flocks. Even when their work involved such barbarous amusements as bullbaiting or dogfighting, they had the dignity of a job to do. It is only in the last century that many breeds of dogs have been reduced from the rank of man's working partners to the status of unemployed pets.

In 1899, the German Shepherd Dog Society was founded, and shepherd fanciers began breeding them for the show ring. The impact of such breeding was to damage the working qualities of the shepherd. More interested in aesthetics than in utility, in appearance than in temperament, show breeders soon produced a shepherd that was elegant to behold, but lacking in the strength, stamina, and mental qualities of a good working dog. Hans von Saarbrücken was not a member of this new breed. He would have been considered old-fashioned, lacking in the refined lines and extreme angulation of the hind legs that appealed to show breeders, but possessing in abundance all the physical and mental characteristics of the worker. Dorothy retained her appreciation of these qualities in spite of changes in her life that followed fast on the acquistion of Hans.

The death of Walter in 1915 made her a widow in her twenties. She continued to live in Hoosick Falls for two years before moving back to Radnor on Philadelphia's Main Line. There in 1923 she married George Eustis of Aiken, South Carolina.

George was closer in age to young Walter than to Dorothy. But age was not their sole discrepancy. George was tall and carelessly handsome. Dorothy was petite and might have seemed plain except for her humorous brown eyes and an engaging directness of manner. She was a born worker. George lived to play. Her joy of life was expressed in an exceptionally merry laugh, but she was motivated by a strong sense of purpose. He was full of animal spirits. One friend describes him as "an utterly charming, utterly attractive rascal."

Young Walter suggests that his mother's awareness of the lack of purpose in her new husband may have prompted an important decision. George Eustis's stepfather was the celebrated concert pianist Josef Hofmann, and Hofmann owned a spectacular chalet on Mt. Pelerin above Vevey in Switzerland. Dorothy proposed to rent the chalet and there to establish a breeding and training kennel to breed back into the German shepherd the working qualities she so valued in Hans. In 1923, she moved with her husband, her sons, and her Hans to Mt. Pelerin and set up the kennels, called Fortunate Fields. Walter says, "I think Mother thought it would give George something to do."

The chalet could have served as a small hotel. One wing was of three stories, the other of four. Both were overrun with balconies and outside staircases with breathtaking views of the lake and mountains beyond. The drawing room held two grand pianos, but could easily have accommodated half a dozen. A visitor wrote, "The house bulges with people: people that work, and guests that play."

George Eustis loved parties and people. His wife's wealth and his stepfather's chalet offered a matchless opportunity to entertain. Since the end of World War I, Europe had become a stamping ground for American expatriates and travelers on the Grand Tour. E. H. Sothern and Julia Marlowe, the matinee idols of their day, had settled nearby. Josef Hofmann was still in residence. There were streams of visitors of the sort that today might be labeled "the beautiful people." Like her husband, Dorothy enjoyed having "heaps of guests," and like Dorothy, George worked in the breeding and training—but there was a difference. For George, it was a kind of game, a game he enjoyed and at which he played hard, but Dorothy's commitment had a religious dimension. It is indicative that in their first year of marriage, she developed an interest in Christian Science while George became knowledgable about wine.

Early in 1928, Dorothy was attracted by some articles on the genetics and breeding of German shepherds published in the *Shepherd Dog Review*. The author was Elliott S. Humphrey, and she began to correspond with him. Humphrey tried to answer the questions with which her letters teemed, but it soon became apparent that he could not tell her what she wanted to know without inspecting her dogs in person. In the end, she offered to pay his way to Switzerland, and he arranged a leave of absence from his job of breeding Arabian horses in Berlin, New Hampshire. He arrived on Mt. Pelerin for the first time in August 1924.

Jack, as Humphrey was generally known, was then thirty-four years old. He was below medium height, with the wiry muscular build and bow legs of a cowboy—which, in fact, he had been. His ears stuck out, and the snuff which he habitually carried between gum and upper lip had earned him the nickname of "the cowboy with the weeping lip." He reminded some people of Will Rogers. There was a leathery charm to his looks. His eyes were gray-blue, and his face was alight with intelligence.

His rearing had been the polar opposite of that of his lady boss. He had been born in Saratoga Springs, New

York, where he worked as an apprentice jockey during the racing season. In his teens he had gone West, where he had driven mules, punched cattle, and broken horses. He had worked as a barker on a sightseeing bus in Los Angeles and entertained tourists to Catalina by diving for abalone shells. He had trained lions and tigers for Diamond Billy Hall, who sold animal acts to circuses, and he once taught a camel to walk backward precisely seventeen steps, an incredible feat which won instant oblivion until the writer Alexander Woollcott resurrected it in a *New Yorker* Profile twenty-five years later.

During the war, he joined the cavalry remount service, purchasing, caring for, and shipping horses. Afterwards he was hired to breed and train Arabians for a millionaire papermaker in New Hampshire. Three times he rode and finished the army's grueling 300-mile endurance race, and once he won it.

Jack Humphrey's brain was even more active than his wiry body. To compensate for his lack of formal schooling, he became an omnivorous reader and an acute observer of everything that went on about him. He had a prodigious memory for what he read and saw. From the study of horse breeding on a New Hampshire farm, he turned to an analysis of the genetics of the German shepherd. It was the publication of his findings in the *Shepherd Dog Review* that brought the Philadelphia blue blood and the cowboy with the weeping lip together.

For all their differences of background, Dorothy Eustis and Jack Humphrey had certain traits in common. Both were strong-willed. Both had keen, active, analytical minds. Both were hard workers, and possibly for this reason, both were attracted to the idea of breeding good working qualities into the shepherd dog. It was not long after his arrival at Fortunate Fields that they agreed to enter into a working partnership for this purpose. Along with his wife Nettie and two-year-old son George, Jack was installed in an apartment in one wing of the chalet, and the experiment at Fortunate Fields began to take on significant shape.

The breeding and training program at Fortunate Fields was unique in several ways. The first of these was its purpose. To Dorothy Eustis, the dog population represented a veritable "Niagara of energy" going to waste because breeders were aiming for beauty instead of utility. Their efforts seemed to her as misguided as converting Niagara Falls into useless fountain displays instead of harnessing it for hydroelectric power. Fortunate Fields was not indifferent to beauty, but it sought to breed as well for the temperament and intelligence that would make dogs useful citizens. Although the German Army alone employed 48,000 working dogs at the end of the war, this was a revolutionary concept at the time. Fortunate Fields was the first systematic attempt to breed for working qualities as well as conformation.

A second peculiar feature was made possible by Dorothy Eustis's wealth. Unlike breeders who depended on the sale of their stock to underwrite their operations, she was financially independent. She need not compromise her standards by breeding the kind of dog that would appeal to the commercial market. She had no interest in selling her dogs.

Jack Humphrey contributed the third distinctive feature of the program: the use of scientific method. He began with a careful analysis of the evidence. Since 1899 the German Shepherd Dog Society had recognized a total of ninety-seven show ring champions and thirty-eight working champions. Jack traced and compared the genealogies of all 135 dogs to identify ancestors common to both types. He found pitifully few. The commercial incentive to breed for the show ring had virtually eliminated working strains, and no breeding stock was available that combined good working qualities with conformation. He would have to begin at the very beginning. He must first define the qualities of the ideal dog Fortunate Fields was seeking and then try to breed for those qualities.

Point by point he defined thirty-five distinct mental and physical characteristics. He assigned each a numerical value based on its desirability and difficulty of attainment. Teachability and endurance rated the highest. He devised a system of compiling a numerical score for each dog's temperament and conformation. The two were then combined into a single number. According to Jack's system, the ideal dog would score 6,720 points.

This ideal dog differed significantly from the standard shepherd of the day. The largeness of size desired in the show ring tended to weaken endurance. Jack preferred a somewhat smaller dog, but one endowed with sufficient strength for its work. The show ring placed a high value on extreme angulation of the hind legs, but Jack found that this tended to be coupled with poor shoulder structure. He preferred sound shoulder structure. He discovered an apparent correlation between the gene for light eyes and that for intelligence. The show ring vogue called for dark eyes. If he were right, breeding for dark eyes would be tantamount to breeding out intelligence.

A good pragmatist, Jack did not permit his theory to blind him to reality. When a dog whose paws he had scored low was able to run almost continuously for twenty-four hours without becoming footsore, he concluded his scoring system was at fault.

It seemed clear to him that the good working qualities of shepherds like Hans had been lost through the practices of line-breeding and in-breeding. Line-breeding matched offspring of the same line. In-breeding was an intensification of line-breeding that mated father with daughter, mother with son, or brother with sister to accentuate certain desirable characteristics. Jack proposed to reverse this process. He would open up bloodlines by breeding dogs who were only distantly related. He sought out and purchased breeding stock of six distinct strains. These, he believed, offered sufficient genetic variety to provide all the characteristics needed for his "ideal dog."

Breeding was only half the program. The puppies must then be raised and put to work. Unlike those of most breeders, puppies whelped at Fortunate Fields were not confined indefinitely in kennel runs where they could learn nothing. After they were weaned, they were literally farmed out to grow up with peasant families in the human society that is so congenial and important for dogs. At four, six, nine, twelve, and fifteen months, they were visited in their foster homes and scored by the Humphrey method. Meticulous records of each dog were updated and carefully filed in the home office.

When they were of a proper age, dogs were brought back to Fortunate Fields and trained for work, since this was the only way of adequately measuring the success of the breeding program. Ultimately, they were graduated into police work, trailing, border patrol, prison duty, military communications, and Red Cross rescue work, but breeding rights were retained for Fortunate Fields.

Jack was already an experienced trainer. George Eustis had considerable natural ability, and he improved it by becoming one of the first civilians ever to take the full four-month course at the Prussian police dog center at Grünheide. A German Swiss with police dog experience, named Mueller, was quartered on the grounds. Dorothy Eustis was too small for hard attack work, but she was active in other phases of the training, and together, they graduated a number of dogs and masters into the police of the Canton de Vaud.

Police dogs must have some instinct for aggression, but it goes against the grain of a mentally balanced dog to attack on command the human beings who have been traditional allies for twenty thousand years. He must be taught to attack. The trainer begins by fluttering a piece of gunnysacking in the dog's face. The dog is eager to please, but cannot figure out what the trainer wants. It may be a matter of days before the worried animal snaps at the gunnysacking in sheer exasperation. Immediately, the trainer showers it with praise to show his approval. When the dog has learned to attack the sacking on command, it is wrapped around the arm of a man in a padded suit.

The desire to please a human master is uniquely canine. In giving intelligence tests, psychologists must motivate all other animals with material rewards of food. Dogs will attempt to solve puzzles set for them "simply because master was inane enough to want them to do it." In *Working Dogs*, a brilliant book that he later wrote with Lucian Warner, Humphrey concluded that although dogs are probably more intelligent than any animal below the primate, it is not their intelligence but their desire to please that makes them so teachable.

Their sensory acuity is advantageous in certain types of work. Dogs are color-blind and cannot see as far or as clearly as humans. If unaided by sound or smell, they fail to recognize their own masters at a short distance, but dogs perceive motion far better than we do. Their hearing is much keener than ours, and their sense of smell is so far superior as to defy comparison. With their noses, they distinguish as many shadings and nuances of scent as our eyes detect in the colors of the rainbow.

At Fortunate Fields, certain traits seemed genetically linked to gender. Males were significantly more aggressive than females, while females were significantly more intelligent than males. At one point, Jack believed he had discovered an inherited reluctance to jump barriers. Since this is an exercise in which dogs generally delight, he was curious and took slow-motion pictures of reluctant dogs jumping. It developed that dogs whose forelegs had too straight an angulation could not break the force of a steep descent and therefore hit their noses when they landed. Their dislike of jumping was due to a structural, not a behavioral, flaw.

Willingness seemed to be inheritable. Wigger von Blasienberg, an outstanding trailing dog purchased in Germany, passed on his trail willingness to no fewer than twenty of his progeny. An interesting genetic phenomenon occurs

when breeds that trail silently are crossed with those that
bay on the scent. The baying gene is dominant, and all the
progeny will trail in cry, but they will take their voice from
the mute parent. Thus, a litter bred from a bloodhound
and a German shepherd would trail in cry like bloodhounds,
barking like shepherds.

Wigger's trailing feats with the Swiss police became
legendary. In his time, he tracked down more than fifty
criminals. He endeared himself to the local peasantry by
trailing and identifying a dog who had been working carnage
on the domesticated chinchillas of neighboring farms. On
another occasion, a peasant discovered he had lost a wallet
containing valuable papers while plowing a two-acre field.
Wigger was called in and began sniffing methodically along
the furrows. In less than half an hour, he stopped, dug down
six inches, and unearthed the wallet. There had been no
way to tell Wigger that it was a wallet he was looking for.
He simply sniffed along until his nose identified something
unusual.

With the constant flow of guests through the chalet on
Mt. Pelerin, tales of Wigger's prowess soon crossed the
Atlantic. When they reached the ear of an alert editor in
Philadelphia, she asked Dorothy Eustis to write an article for
the *Saturday Evening Post*. As Jack recalled, "This request
probably had in mind a story of the work being done at
Fortunate Fields. To have written such a story would at
that time have caused a lot of inquiry to buy Fortunate
Fields dogs, when none were for sale, as they were being
trained, put to work, and breeding rights retained for future
breeding use. To have sold them to come to the States could
have resulted in a loss of animals which would later be
needed for our breeding program. As a result, Dorothy
decided on the story of what the Germans had done for
their war blind."

With her deepening involvement in Christian Science,
it is not surprising that Dorothy Eustis chose her title from
the Bible. A verse in *Proverbs* reads: "The seeing eye and

the hearing ear, the Lord hath made even both of them."
She called her article "The Seeing Eye."

She chose her subject so as to deflect publicity from
Fortunate Fields and to avoid nuisance mail from American
shepherd breeders. She succeeded in her immediate object,
but her article had other, wholly unforeseen consequences.

CHAPTER 2

"The Seeing Eye"

GUIDE DOGS for the blind are not new. A blind Germanic king is supposed to have had a guide dog in 100 B.C. A wall painting in Pompeii depicts what seems to be a blind man whose dog is leading him through the marketplace. The blind Saint Herve is said to have been led all around Brittany by a small white dog in the sixth century. A thirteenth-century Chinese scroll shows a dog leading its blind master, and there are manuscript references to guide dogs in Western Europe in the same period.

From the fifteenth century on, there were a great many drawings and paintings of blind men with their dogs, including those by Tintoretto, Rembrandt, and Gainsborough. They share many features in common. The dogs are too small to pull their masters out of harm's way. They guide with flexible leashes which could indicate only a general direction. The masters carry long staffs or canes. All are men, and all seem to be wandering beggars or musicians. The general impression is depressing, and the guidance is ineffective. Occasionally a dog is shown leading its master into a ditch or looking on as he falls from a bridge.

Presumably, these dogs were trained by their blind

masters. For the first time in 1819, Father Johann Klein, a Viennese priest, proposed that guide dogs should be trained by sighted instructors. He pointed out that a rigid leading stick attached to the dog's harness would give a much more accurate sense of its movements than a flexible leash. He gave a brief description of how dogs might be trained and recommended shepherds and poodles for the work.

So far as we know, there was no attempt to establish a systematic school for guide dogs for nearly a century after Father Klein's suggestion. In 1916, the manpower shortage of the war made it difficult to provide human guides for blind German veterans. A systematic effort to train German shepherds as guides was begun at Oldenburg. Its success led to the opening of a second school at Württemberg. Following the war, schools for dogs to guide the civilian blind were established at Potsdam and Munich. By the time Dorothy Eustis's article appeared, there may have been as many as 4,000 Germans using guide dogs.

Dorothy had known of the work in Germany for several years. Too often the story has been told as if the discovery of the Potsdam school had come as a dazzling revelation which she immediately sought to share with the American people. As early as January 1924, a certain Herr Schwanatus had written a detailed account of German guide dogs in a letter to George. In that same year, Dorothy had offered the American Red Cross to pay for the cost of bringing a German dog and trainer to the United States. She and George had visited the Potsdam school in 1925 and 1926.

The German work had been brought to the attention of American workers for the blind long before Dorothy's *Post* article was published. In 1923, the American Association of Workers for the Blind heard a lecture on guide dog schooling by a German trainer. In 1925, the Potsdam school offered Robert Irwin of the American Foundation for the Blind to provide both dogs and trainers for a fee. John L.

Synikin, a Minneapolis dog breeder, studied the work in Germany and returned to set up the Master Eye Foundation. He imported a German-trained dog which he retrained for Senator Thomas Schall of Minnesota in 1927. At about the same time, Josef Weber, who had worked with both police dogs and guide dogs in his native Germany, was establishing a training kennel outside Princeton, New Jersey.

Yet none of these early efforts interested workers for the blind in America. They had formed an image of guiding work very much like that depicted in the paintings of earlier centuries. Edward Allen, head of the prestigious Perkins School for the Blind, characterized it as of "a dirty little cur dragging a blind man along at the end of a string, the very index of incompetence and beggary." Robert Irwin at the American Foundation said he "would not be caught with one of the blooming things." The preconceptions of professional workers for the blind obscured their perception of the new image presented in Dorothy Eustis's article, but the article was addressed to the general public rather than to professionals in the field. The professionals had convinced themselves that guide dogs would not work. The public had a more open mind. Readers were gripped by the article's opening lines:

> To everyone, I think, there is always something particularly pathetic about a blind man. Shorn of his strength and his independence, he is prey to all the sensitiveness of his position and he is at the mercy of all with whom he comes in contact. The sensitiveness, above all, is an almost insuperable obstacle to cope with, in his fight for a new life, for life goes on willy-nilly and the new conditions must be reckoned with. In darkness and uncertainty he must start again, wholly dependent on outside help for every move. His other senses may rally to his aid, but they cannot replace his eyesight. To man's never failing friend has been accorded this special privilege. Gentleman, I give you the German shepherd dog!

Because of their extraordinary intelligence and fidelity, Germany has chosen her own breed of shepherd dog to help her in the rehabilitation of her war blind, and in the lovely city of Potsdam she has established a very simple and businesslike school for training her dogs as blind leaders.

Enclosed with a high board fence, the school consists of dormitories for the blind, kennels for the dogs, and quarters for the teachers, the different buildings framing a large park laid out in sidewalks and roads with curbs, steps, bridges, and obstacles of all kinds, such as scaffoldings, barriers, telephone poles, and ditches, everything, in fact, that a blind man has to cope with in everyday life.

The article then described the various stages of guide-dog education over a four-month period. The total cost of a dog trained and ready to leave the school was only sixty dollars. The guide was able to transmit signals to its blind master through a semi-rigid, U-shaped, leather handle attached to the harness. A dog learned to pull back before curbs until its master could find the edge with his cane, to stop before approaching traffic, and to swerve around trees or pedestrians.

Up to this point in the article, readers must have been interested, but incredulous. Dorothy Eustis anticipated her readers' skepticism by proclaiming her own.

I had seen so many so-called trained dogs which, put to the test, did mediocre work accompanied by many excuses that I was more or less prepared to hear reasons for poor work. I had expected possibly to see an instructor with eyes bandaged give an exhibtion with one special dog to the running accompaniment of "He's off his work today—didn't eat this morning; he was not exercised yesterday; that's funny, he usually does that perfectly; there must be something distracting him," and so on. . . . I had read of the blind man who crosses the Potsdamer Platz in Berlin with his dog twice a day, going to and from work, and had seen a photograph of him there, but knowing how much the Potsdamer Platz would resemble Fifth Avenue and Forty-second Street if all the traffic were allowed to circulate at the same time, I put it down to a good story and a better photograph. Consequently, I was not prepared to have one little incident open wide the door to my conversion.

She described a class of blind men shuffling and groping uncertainly down a path to a gate where they called their dogs for harnessing.

I shall never forget the change that came over one man as he turned away from that gate. It was as though a complete transformation had taken place before my eyes. One moment it was an uncertain, shuffling blind man, tapping with a cane, the next it was an assured person, with his dog firmly in hand and his head up, who walked toward us quickly and firmly, giving his orders in a low, confident voice. That one quick glimpse of the crying need for guidance and companionship in the lonely, all-enveloping darkness stood out clearly before my swimming eyes. To think that one small dog could stand for so much in the life of a human being, not only with his usual role of companion but as his eyes, sword, shield, and buckler! How many humans could fill those roles with the same uncomplaining devotion and untiring fidelity? Darned few, I think! . . .

As I followed him, it seemed impossible to believe that the man wasn't taking the dog for a walk and stopping for traffic on his own accord. . . . Not once through the whole hour that I followed them did that dog's attention wander. The walk lay through the crowded shopping street with all the traffic of a big city, its noises, distractions, its scents, and stray dogs on mischief or business bent. . . .

As he threaded his way along the street, and the pair went much more quickly without interference than I, who continually bumped into people in my attempt to keep up, I was amazed at the pace; I had started by walking briskly, but I found the distance ever widening and the need to make it up every so often on a jog trot.

The most critical test came when the man and dog entered a path which had barriers constructed to keep out cyclists. The bicycle barriers were broken here and there by narrow openings to admit pedestrians. Since the barriers were waist-high, it would be easy for the dog to walk beneath a bar that would catch his master in the midriff.

> A couple strolling ahead had dropped a coat directly in the path, but the man and dog skirted it and the dog immediately came back to a line that would lead him between the barriers, although for him it would have been simpler and shorter to go under.
>
> There was a big catch in my throat as I saw them turn into the school grounds with other pairs coming from different directions and I knew that I was converted.
>
> It had not been a particular exhibition staged for my special benefit, but just one of the many dogs turned out every month with its blind master. There were no fireworks, no display, no excuses, no muddling, but honest work done by honest dogs, and my hat was off to those who had worked out and perfected such a method of sympathetic training.

After describing a meeting with another blind man who had had his dog for three whole years without bumping into anything except once, when it was the master's fault, Dorothy Eustis concluded with a fanfare:

> The future for all blind men can be the same, however blinded. No longer dependent on a member of the family, a friend, or a paid attendant, the blind can once more take up their normal lives as nearly as possible where they left them off, and each can begin or go back to a wage-earning occupation, secure in the knowledge that he can get to and from his work safely and without cost; that crowds and traffic have no longer any terrors for him and that his evenings can be spent among friends without responsibility or burden to them; and last but far from least, that long, healthful walks are now possible to exercise off the unhealthy fat of inactivity and so keep the body strong and

fit. Gentlemen, again without reservation, I give you the shepherd dog!

Dorothy had written the article, sent it to America, and dismissed it from her thoughts. Toward the end of the summer of 1927, she and George, her sons, Walter, now twenty, and Harrison, thirteen, and her orphaned niece and ward, Esther Rowland, had spent a month in Venice. On their return to Fortunate Fields, they were joined by Jack Humphrey, who had been in the States winding up his final obligations to his former employer in Berlin, New Hampshire. He was now free of all concerns but the management of Fortunate Fields. Both he and she were looking forward eagerly to the work ahead, but a rude shock awaited them.

The *Post* published "The Seeing Eye" on November 5. The reaction was immediate and unexpected. As Jack put it, "What had not been thought of was the fact that it would be read to the blind. Soon, bundles of letters came to Dorothy from the Curtis Publishing Company, letters from the blind, mostly on one theme: 'Is this story true? If it is true, where can I get a dog? I am blind.' "

Dorothy had written about Potsdam to divert the attention of dog fanciers from Fortunate Fields, but her strategy had backfired. Jack walked into the big room one day to find her at her desk, crying. When he asked what was wrong, she said, "Jack, what have I done? I have shown the American blind there is a way to liberty and raised their hopes, when there is no way they can have the liberty we have shown them."

She had brought Jack Humphrey to Fortunate Fields to make its program a scientific experiment. Now the demands of humanity were intruding. Was science deaf to humanity? Were the two incompatible?

As Dorothy Eustis wrestled with these questions, her

attention was drawn to another letter. It was written on the stationery of The National Life and Accident Insurance, Inc., Nashville, Tennessee, addressed to the Curtis Publishing Company, and dated November 9, 1927. The first two paragraphs are quoted here:

My dear Mrs. Eustis,
In reference to your article "The All Seeing Eye" which appeared in the Saturday Evening Post of November 5th, is of great interest to me so that is the reason why I take the liberty to address this letter to you.

I have often thought of this solution for the blind but have never heard of it being put to a practical use before, of course there are a few cases throughout the United States realizing that if handled in the proper manner and supervised correctly this would be quite a help to the blind of our country. I would appreciate very much if you would be kind enough to give me more information upon this matter and if you would give me the address of this school in Germany, or of any trainer in this country who might have anything similar as I should like very much to forward this work in this country, as three and a half years ago at the age of sixteen I was deprived of my sight and know from practical experience what rehabilitation means and what it means to be dependent upon a paid helper who are unsympathetic and not interested in their work and do not appreciate kindness as shown to them and as you well know that there are many throughout the land who not even have paid attendants.

The letter was signed "Morris S. Frank." As the reader can see, it is rambling and almost without punctuation. Its opening sentence gives the wrong title for the article. Although the writer mentions that he "should like very much to forward this work in this country," this can hardly be considered a pledge of commitment, especially in the context of the structureless sentence in which it appears. Yet for some reason, Dorothy Eustis, herself a stickler for clarity of expression, sensed something special in this garbled message from a nineteen-year-old in Nashville. Was it second sight, dumb luck, or Divine Providence? Whatever it was, it is certain that, of all the people who had written her, no one was so well equipped for the role he would play in the creation of The Seeing Eye as Morris S. Frank.

CHAPTER 3

Southern
Rebel

MORRIS FRANK was born in Nashville on March 23, 1908, the third and much the youngest son of well-to-do parents. John Frank was the typical Southern gentleman, soft-spoken, suave, courteous. Jessie Hirsch Frank was a fighter who had imbibed a passion for social reform from her Jewish heritage.

She lost the sight of one eye when it hemorrhaged during the birth of her first son. Some fifteen years later on the Fourth of July, she was riding horseback when a boy threw a firecracker beneath her horse. She was thrown and stunned. On returning to consciousness, she was totally blind.

Blindness did not dull her social conscience. "Every day of her life," Morris says, she made three baby nightgowns for distribution through the settlement house she had helped to found in Nashville. She knew the leading social workers in Chicago's Hull House and New York's Henry Street Settlement and was active in the Council of Jewish Women. She was an ardent supporter of Margaret Sanger and birth control. Morris remembers George Washington Carver at the family dinner table at a time when interracial dining was taboo. Other houseguests were the prison reformer and warden of Sing Sing, Thomas Mott

Osborne, and such leaders of work for the blind as Edward
Van Cleve of the New York Institute for the Blind, Edward
Allen of the Perkins School for the Blind, and Olin Burritt
of the Philadelphia School for the Blind.

As far back as Morris can remember, his mother was
blind, and he was her helper from an early age. He recalls
being her sole traveling companion and guide on a trip to
Maine when he was only six. By that time, he had already
lost one eye to an overhanging limb while riding horseback.
At sixteen, he was sparring with friends on a school play-
ground when a fist caught him squarely in the other eye.
He never saw again.

His early apprenticeship with his mother had prepared
him for some aspects of blindness. Its conspicuousness did
not bother him in the least, but he was active and impatient by nature and he resented his lack of freedom. In
1924, services for the blind were relatively meager, and
Morris's prospects were bleak. There was no classes for
cane travel, and there would be no scientific attempt to
develop cane technique until World War II. What Morris
learned about the use of the cane, he taught himself. Following World War I, the white cane had been introduced
in France and had later spread to England, but it was almost
unknown in America. The first city ordinance to offer users
of the white cane the right of way was passed in Peoria,
Illinois, in 1930.

The education of blind children was well established
in 1924. The Perkins School had been chartered by the
Massachusetts legislature in 1829. The New York Institute
and Philadelphia School came hard on its heels, but schools
segregated blind children from the sighted world, and
Perkins had been established as the "New England Asylum
for the Blind." When Morris went blind, many schools were
still called "asylums."

Louis Braille had invented his coded alphabet in 1829,
but so many attempts were made to improve on it that there
was a sort of Babel in embossed type. Until 1917, when an

international conference agreed on a single system, books for the blind were being transcribed in five different codes. For some time there had been a small federal subsidy for embossing texts for schoolchildren, but there would be no subsidy for embossing adult books until 1931, and Talking Book records were still further in the future.

In 1924, the American Foundation for the Blind was only three years old, and there were few special aids and devices. There were no braille watches, for example. Morris was given a pocket repeater, bought for him in Europe. When he pressed a spring, it chimed the hours, quarter-hours, and minutes. The mechanism was cunning, but far beyond the means of the average blind person and less efficient than a watch with braille numbers fixed to its face.

Significant work for the adult blind had begun around the turn of the century. States with commissions for the blind employed itinerant instructors to teach braille in their clients' homes. Sheltered workshops offered blind men and women an opportunity to earn money instead of begging on street corners or depending on the support of their families; but segregation, like stagnation, breeds its own poison, and charity could become despotic. For example, Mrs. Quinan, the director of a sheltered workshop in San Francisco, was so jealous of her little domain that she refused Helen Keller permission to set foot inside.

It was Helen Keller who said that "not blindness, but the attitude of the seeing to the blind is the hardest burden to bear." Fifty years ago, agencies for the blind viewed their clients as helpless. The phrase "for the Blind" in so many agency titles implied this helplessness. Blindness was supposed to be so terrible a handicap that it wiped out all individual distinctions in those it "afflicted." There could be no blind individuals. "The Blind" were homogenized as a class, reduced to their lowest common denominator. After graduating from Princeton in 1906, Mervyn Sinclair spent many years as an executive in the family business until a hunting accident blinded him at the age of thirty-nine.

When he consulted an agency for guidance, he found that his education and his executive experience counted for nothing. He was blind. "The Blind" make brooms. He was offered a job in the broom shop.

Morris had been exposed to many important workers for the blind, but he did not share the prevailing philosophy. He did not consider blind people helpless, and he was far too full of himself to accept classification as one of "the Blind." He was a rebel who possessed the courage of his impetuous convictions to an unusual degree. Offered a job making brooms, he determined to sell insurance instead. He also enrolled in Vanderbilt University. Several months before, he had given up after two weeks studying braille with a home teacher, but finding that he needed it for business and college, he taught it to himself.

Looking back, Morris feels he was especially fortunate in having a group of loyal school friends who included him in their social activities without patronizing and who refused to let him exploit his handicap. One night at a country club dance when he had had too much to drink, he got into an argument with a boy who did not know he was blind. Morris challenged him to a fight. One of his friends immediately stepped in to do battle on Morris's behalf, but afterwards, Morris recalls, "They took me out on the green and beat the hell out of me for getting drunk and acting like a son of a bitch." At Vanderbilt, "Every time I came out of a class, there was always a friend who just happened to be going where I was going. It wasn't until years later that it finally dawned on me that those wonderful bastards had worked it out between themselves without letting me catch on."

He was not so lucky with paid guides. He was attending the university only part-time. For his business, he hired young blacks to lead him. They were frequently late and sometimes failed to show up at all. One boy demanded a raise when they were out on the street. When Morris refused, he abandoned him in the midst of the business district. This was what Morris meant in his letter to Dorothy Eustis when he said he knew "what it means to be dependent upon a paid helper." The thought of the freedom of movement a guide dog would offer fired his imagination.

He wrote to a number of his mother's connections among workers for the blind to ask their opinions of the guide dog. Their responses were universally discouraging, but Morris refused to be discouraged, and his hopes soared when he heard from Mrs. Eustis at last. She explained that she was a Philadelphian living in Switzerland. Although her kennel had produced many working dogs, it had never attempted training a dog to lead a blind man. However, she had a man who might be able to train one for Morris. She would be home in Philadelphia for the Christmas holidays and would be in touch with him again.

Morris answered immediately. He began, "I have some good news for you. Senator Smutz of Minnesota" (he meant Senator Schall) "has purchased a dog from Munich which was trained in German, but is now being retrained in English and is proving absolutely satisfactory to our sightless Senator, taking him all over Washington. I believe that in a month after I have the dog, I can train it to take me anywhere in the United States."

He continued, "Now if it would be possible for you to bring one of these dogs with you already trained, I should be very glad to send you either a banker's check or money by the American Express or any way you so desire, because I hope in the winter to make my eastern trip, and then I will be able to get in touch with the leaders of the blind work in the United States. I have the honor and privilege through my mother of being personally acquainted with Charles Campbell, who is head of the blind soldiers at Evergreen, the United States Hospital for blind soldiers." He added that he was also acquainted with Allen at Perkins, Van Cleve at the New York Institute, "and many other notable leaders of this great work, and I believe we can show them where this is feasible."

If there was any red tape about importing the dog, he begged her to let him know, "so that I may be able to bring to bear any political influence that my family may be able to have." Dorothy Harrison Eustis must have smiled at this offer of political influence from a boy of nineteen, but she admired both his initiative and his altruism. He wanted a dog not only for himself, but for all blind Americans, and he was willing to work for it. She cabled him that there was no possibility of bringing a dog on this trip and followed with a letter of explanation.

Morris's reply accepted the delay with the thought that "there is absolutely no use in rushing our work." The "our" suggests that he has graciously taken her into partnership. He again listed a number of workers for the blind who knew his mother and added that Senator Schall had not done nearly so well with his dog as he had at first supposed. In fact, his difficulties had hurt the cause of the guide dog among the workers for the blind. "Of course, you and I know that this is as much the Senator's fault as the dog's, but I am confident that, with a good demonstration, this objection can be quickly overruled."

Arriving in the United States, Dorothy made her own contacts with leaders for the blind. Despite Morris's claims of friendship, Charles Campbell, now with the Detroit League for the Blind, could not recall Mrs. Frank. A letter from the National Society for the Prevention of Blindness complimented Mrs. Frank on her work as chairman of the Council of Jewish Women, Department of the Blind, but regretted that, since the society dealt only with prevention, "we cannot give you any guidance." Mr. Allen at Perkins described Mrs. Frank as "a lady whose delight seems to be in social service" and Morris as "a fine young fellow," but offered no assistance. Olin Burritt at the Philadelphia, later the Overbrook, School was distinctly cool.

The New York Lighthouse sidestepped Dorothy's approach by referring her instead to the American Foundation for the Blind. She called on Robert Irwin and promised that, if the foundation would sponsor a guide dog program, she and George would come to New York with a string of dogs from Fortunate Fields and would spend four months training the dogs, teaching a pair of instructors, and supervising the adjustment of a class of blind people and dogs. All this she would do at her own expense, provided the foundation would carry on the program from there. She estimated that a pair of instructors working full-time could turn out from sixty to seventy dogs and masters annually at a cost of no more than $150 per unit.

Irwin agreed to put her proposition before the executive committee late in January. If he had coupled his presentation with his wholehearted approval, the committee might have accepted her offer and the history of the guide dog movement in America would have been radically changed. But Irwin had already rejected two earlier offers from the Potsdam school, and he may have had subjective reasons for distrusting guide dogs. His was a first-rate mind, but physically Irwin has been described by a colleague as "the blindest man I ever saw." Conscious that he lacked the coordination and sense of orientation to work a guide dog himself, he may have projected his own limitations upon the blind population as a whole.

A cultural factor may also have had a negative influence. As a nation, Germans understood, appreciated, and trusted the working capacity of dogs. As a nation, Americans did not. With exceptions, especially among the hunting breeds, most American dogs were pampered, undisciplined pets, far from the "useful citizens" turned out at Fortunate Fields. Those who were unfamiliar with responsible working dogs would be naturally wary of trusting blind people to their care.

In some quarters, too, the German shepherd had an unsavory reputation. Following the war, shepherds had been imported from Germany, and a number that had been trained for police or guard work became the property of inexperienced masters. A dog with attack training in the hands of a novice is potentially as dangerous as a loaded revolver in the hands of a child. Some ugly accidents had resulted, and the German shepherd gained an undeserved reputation for viciousness.

If a generalized distrust or ignorance of dogs undermined the confidence of many agency heads, there were also financial difficulties in Dorothy's proposal to Irwin. Generous as was her contribution, she was expecting the foundation to assume a highly experimental program which, by her own estimate, would cost roughly $10,000 a year. In any case, Irwin did not endorse her proposal to the foundation's executive committee, and it was politely declined.

Dorothy Eustis set her small jaw. She had spent a full month trying to interest American agencies in the virtues of the guide dog, and everywhere she had encountered the negative weight of inertia. That a man as physically blind and groping as Robert Irwin should refuse the opportunity to experience the confidence and security she had seen and described at Potsdam was galling. His negativism was in sharp contrast to the ebullient affirmation of the brash young man in Nashville.

On the night of Feburary 9, she placed a long-distance call to Morris. He listened in rising excitement to the words spoken in a cultivated Philadelphia accent. She offered to pay his fare to Switzerland and to train him there with a dog. "Would you be willing to travel all the way to Switzerland for a dog?"

Morris nearly shouted his answer into the mouthpiece. "Mrs. Eustis, to get my independence back, I'd go to hell!"

The following morning, he wrote her a long letter. "I can arrange to leave at any time that is convenient for you and naturally under any conditions you think best, but as I am accustomed to traveling alone, I would really prefer it." He outlined his preparations, asked for any books on dogs or dog training she would recommend, and expressed his confidence in the future success of the guide dog movement in a burst of cliché. "I believe this work can be put over by good hard work, for my motto is and always has been, 'A winner never quits, and a quitter never wins!' "

Dorothy's original plan had been to buy from the Potsdam school two already trained dogs which Jack and her husband would then polish and turn over to Morris Frank and another blind American, Howard Buchanan of Monmouth, Illinois. Buchanan had gone blind several years before while working as a missionary doctor in the Sudan. Dorothy always liked having a second string to her bow, and she felt that Dr. Buchanan could supply the maturity and experience that young Morris lacked.

Her hopes failed to materialize. Potsdam refused to sell her the dogs, so Jack and George were forced to make time in their crowded schedules to teach guiding to a pair of Fortunate Fields dogs. Both had seen enough of German schools to have a grasp of basic principles, and Jack was a genius with animals, but they had to feel their way, and they had less than the three months the Germans customarily allotted to prepare a dog. A second difficulty developed when Dr. Buchanan was forced to cancel his trip to Switzerland on account of illness. Temporarily at least, Dorothy would have to confide the fate of the American guide dog movement solely into the hands of the young rebel from Nashville.

Travel arrangements for Morris were delegated to Dorothy's personal secretary, Gretchen Green. Of the entire cast of characters connected with the origins of The Seeing Eye, Miss Green was the most implausible. Both picturesque and picaresque, she was a sort of feminine Don Quixote, except that she was anything but melancholy and so extraordinarily resourceful that her adventures seemed always to end in triumph.

Gretchen grew up as the daughter of a clergyman with pulpits in Alabama, Missouri, Kansas, Tennessee, and Maine. She began adult life as a social worker in Philadelphia, but her later peregrinations took her to five continents, and she was completely at home wherever she went. Among other things, she was a Big Sister in New York and the director of a woman's clinic at the University of Tagore in India. As an advance agent for Malvina Hoffman, the sculptor, on an expedition in search for racial types, she traveled throughout the Orient. During World War II, she ran a Camel Corps Canteen for the British in North Africa.

She was nearly six feet tall, with sloping shoulders and an unnaturally sunken chest resulting from a crippling accident in childhood. She walked with the lope of a camel, dressed floridly with long loops of showy beads, and always wore the bishop's ring she had inherited from her grandfather. Without pretensions to wealth, social position, or beauty, she commanded immense influence by her charm, humor, energy, and just plain goodness.

People who knew her are likely to recall her with a warm smile and one of three opening remarks: "Gretchen knew *everybody!*" "Gretchen could do *anything!*" "Gretchen would do *anything* for *anybody!*" She would arrange to have your daughter presented at the Court of St. James's, but her generosity overflowed class distinctions, and she knew how to "walk with kings, nor lose the common touch." In Paris, where she saw Lindbergh land, she had a chance encounter with a gendarme. Discovering, as only she could have, that he was trying to improve his English, she contrived, as only she knew how, to have him transferred to a quarter with many English and American residents. Once, staying in a Chinese hotel, she had a call from a man who chanced to recognize her name on the hotel register. He was currently studying to be a Buddhist monk, but had last seen Gretchen many years before when he was being held in the lockup in Boise, Idaho, where Gretchen was a policewoman.

At the time Dorothy Eustis met her, she was running a teahouse in Venice. As a favor to a friend, the former British ambassador to Turkey, Gretchen had agreed to find a tenant for his *palazzo*. Dorothy became the tenant. It was the summer of 1927. Walter recalls, "Mother and Gretchen

were as different as day and night, but they got on famously."
When Dorothy and her party returned to Mt. Pelerin in the
fall, Gretchen went along as her personal sceretary and good
right hand.

Gretchen's solution for a blind man traveling alone
from New York to Vevey had the simplicity of genius. She
shipped him like a parcel by American Express. That solved
Gretchen's problem, but not Morris Frank's. The Cunard
Line steward who took him in charge for the crossing treated
him like a precious but unpredictable pet dog. He led him
to the dining room for feeding for breakfast, lunch, and
dinner, trotted him around the deck for exercise, and sat
him in a deck chair for the rest of the day. He would probably have liked to strap him in, for if Morris dared to leave
his chair to meet and mingle with the other passengers, his
hawk-eyed guardian seized him by the elbow and firmly
returned him to his place. After dinner, he was allowed to
socialize briefly in the lounge, where he met a delightful
English girl, but at nine o'clock sharp, he was led off to his
cabin and locked in for the night.

Consoling himself on his blindness, the poet John
Milton wrote, "They also serve who only stand and wait,"
but such words were no consolation to Morris on landing at
Le Havre. In the customs shed, he was told to stand and
wait until he was fetched for the Paris train. He stood and
waited. As he listened to voices on all sides shouting mean-
ingless sounds, he was seized with a sudden panic. In this
foreign land where he could neither speak nor understand
the language, he was not only blind, but deaf and dumb as
well. He dared not move for fear of being run down by the
clattering luggage barrows of hurrying porters. All he could
do was stand and wait. He had never felt so helpless in his
life.

After an infinity of waiting, a representative of American Express boarded him on the train for the city of wine,
women, and song. For Morris, it offered one woman and one
bottle of wine, but no song. The woman, a French employee

of American Express, guided him directly to a hotel room, showed him a bottle of wine, and locked him in with it. It was ironical, Morris thought, that throughout this trip designed to regain his freedom, he had been a closely guarded prisoner. He drank the wine and lay down to doze until American Express shook him awake to catch the midnight train to Vevey. He arrived on the morning of April 25, 1928.

Mrs. Eustis and Jack Humphrey met him at the station. They had seen a portrait photograph of Morris. It showed a dark, handsome, young face with generous, even features and a mouth that looked ready to smile. What concerned them far more than his face was his physique and coordination. They scanned him closely. He was a six-footer of medium build. When they introduced themselves, he looked directly at them and would not have appeared blind except for his posture. During the years of groping and straining to hear, he had developed a forward thrust of his head. However, they had seen similarly hanging heads on the new students in Potsdam, and they had soon straightened up with their dogs. This young man walked better than most, picking up his feet, and he showed good orientation as he climbed into the back of the Rolls.

Morris was equally curious about Mrs. Eustis and Jack. He noted her small, firm hand and Jack's strong, hard one, her clear, low voice and Jack's big laugh. Jack was adept in guiding him to the limousine, and he noted that neither of them raised their voices to him in the infuriating way so many people did, as if he were deaf instead of blind. Mrs. Eustis was direct and friendly, but he sensed something formidable about her. When she spoke to the chauffeur in French, her voice carried a quiet tone of command that was unmistakable. This, he thought, was a dame who liked to have her own way.

After his experience in France, it was good to hear English, even with Yankee accents, but as they neared the top of the mountain, his hostess embarrassed him with a reversion to French. On the gates of the property, she said, was a sign that read, *"Prenez garde aux chiens, et s'addressez à la ferme vis-à-vis."* One of her guests had translated it, "Take care of the dogs and address them with a firm face." Morris was quick and he joined in the laughter, but he had no idea what she was talking about.

During the next five weeks, Morris experienced a series of emotions and sensations that would be repeated with variations literally thousands of times in the future. They ranged from strangeness to confusion, anxiety to exhilaration, depression to exasperation, fear to anger to panic, love to laughter to triumph. Strangeness and uncertainty came first. The vastness of the chalet was bewildering. The dining room was on the second floor. Below it, the huge drawing room was entered hazardously down three steps. Although the Eustises and Humphreys spoke English, their conversation referred to so many things beyond his experience that it was difficult to follow. He was travel-weary, and it was a relief to retreat to the safety of his bedroom for a good night's sleep.

After he had gone, Jack and George conferred. Because Dr. Buchanan had postponed his trip, they had two dogs to choose from, Gala and Kiss. Both dogs were good and willing workers, but Kiss was imperturbable as well. The dog that pioneered the way across America with Morris would need nerves of steel. Kiss had them. They settled on her.

When they told Morris at breakfast the next morning, the name horrified him. Kiss! Imagine what the gang at home would say. Kiss! He would be the laughingstock of the campus.

The meeting with her came right after breakfast. Jack took Morris to his room and explained that the first thing he must do was to make friends with his dog. Pat her. Talk to her. Play with her. Make it pleasant for her to be with him. Then he gave Morris a piece of raw meat to give her on meeting and went off to fetch her from the kennels. Morris sat in a chair with the raw meat in his palm, waiting. After a long time, he heard Jack's footsteps approaching. They were accompanied by the jingle of a chain collar. The door opened.

"Here, girl!" Morris called. His tone was coaxing, but he refused to use the awful name. Claws clicked across the floor. He opened his hand. A cool, wet nose sniffed. Then he felt the lap of a warm tongue, and she began eating daintily. He ran his free hand over her warm fur, the contours of her head and shoulders from the erect velvet ears down to the bushy tail, swooping in a graceful S curve. She was beautiful. The tail waved slightly.

"Kiss!" he growled under his breath. "That's a hell of a name for a dog. I'm going to call you Buddy."

When the ceremony of introduction was over, Jack showed Morris a leash and harness and explained their use. The leash was a leather strap about four feet long with a metal clip at either end. He let Morris feel it. One clip was for the dog's collar; the other could be doubled over and snapped to a ring at the other end to make a short leash. If it were snapped to another ring a foot from the master's end, it formed a convenient loop for the hand as a long leash. Jack had Morris practice changing from short to long leash several times before showing him the harness.

The harness consisted of three straps. One vertical strap ran over the dog's shoulders and buckled under the rib cage. It was sewn at the shoulders to a horizontal strap running across the chest. From the center of the chest strap, a third strap or martingale ran between the dog's front legs and ended in a loop through which the first strap was passed before buckling. As an experienced horseman, Morris was familiar with a martingale, but when Jack asked him to harness and unharness Buddy, it was not as simple as he had imagined. If he miscalculated the position of Buddy's head, he could catch the chest strap on her nose, pinch her ear, or put a finger in her eye.

By means of metal clips, a loop of heavy leather was attached to the harness at Buddy's shoulders. When he worked Buddy, he would hold this loop in his left hand. Since it was more than eighteen inches long, it would position Buddy well in front of him. In addition to the harness handle, his left hand would hold the short leash looped around his middle and ring fingers. If he dropped the harness handle for any reason, he would still have Buddy on short leash. His right hand would hold a cane.

Morris was impatient to try it at once, but Jack said he would have to wait. A guide dog works for the praise of the master it loves. It would take time to win Buddy's affection, and for the first twenty-four hours he must give her a chance to get accustomed to him. When he moved around, Buddy was to walk with him at heel on short leash. Today and from now on, he must personally feed Buddy twice a day and take her out to empty four times. A staircase from the balcony outside Morris's bedroom led to a stretch of lawn for this purpose. Even at meals, he must keep Buddy on leash, lying out of the way under the table, with Morris's foot over the end of the leash near her collar and the other end over his knee.

Being leashed to Buddy every waking moment did not improve Morris's freedom of movement, and his attempts to make friends with her were frustrating. He had imagined himself with a devoted and fun-loving Rin-Tin-Tin, a dog whose tail would wag furiously at a word from him, who would be eager to lick his hands and face, always ready for a roughhouse. This Buddy was beautiful, but aloof. She tolerated his caresses, but the only time she showed any genuine enthusiasm was when George or Jack came in the room. Then she jumped to her feet and thumped her tail hard against his leg. When he went to bed that night and felt the cool Alpine air pouring in through the window, he called Buddy up on the bed and dropped off to sleep aware of her warm, furry bulk beside him.

The next morning Morris had his first real glimpse

into what a guide dog could mean. To anyone trying it for the first time, working a guide dog is a thrilling new form of locomotion, as different from ordinary walking as skiing, skating, or riding a bicycle. Like them, it requires a different set of physical responses. There is a fluid quality to it. The harness handle seems alive, vibrant with the rhythm of the dog's shoulders pulling hard. The sensation of speed is intense. You catch your breath. You feel half uncertain, half triumphant, as if you were just learning to fly. Wendy, John, and Michael may have felt something very like it when Peter Pan taught them to ride the back of the wind.

Morris felt it with Buddy that April morning on Mt. Pelerin. Buddy had been taught to walk much faster and pull much harder than the guide dogs of today. The rigid U-shaped harness handle introduced a few years later gave an accurate clue to a dog's position even when it was standing still, but the flexible strap attached to Buddy's harness required a hard pull to give a clear sense of direction. At four miles an hour, Morris had never walked so fast before. His stride lengthened and his spine straightened. He was flying along. A radiant smile spread across his face.

But this was work, not play. Jack followed close behind Morris and Buddy with a running fire of instructions. "Don't grip the harness. Let your thumb hang free. . . ." A moment later "Follow your dog. She's trying to lead you left. . . ." Then, "Your harness hand is riding forward. Straighten up. . . ." And after a little silence, "In a few steps she's going to stop. Be ready to stop with her. Good! Reward your dog. Now you're at a curb. Feel with your cane. Which is it? A step up or a step down?"

Morris discovered that there was a right and a wrong way to do everything. He was expected not only to know the right way, but the reason why it was right. The commands of "left" and "right" were to be accompanied by precise hand signals and body movements. At curbs, Morris was to position himself with right foot on the edge and left foot back. At the command "Buddy, right," he must gesture right with his right hand, turn his body ninety degrees, and move his right foot back from the curb to offer Buddy free passage. Commands must be given in a clear, firm voice, and every command obeyed, every service performed must be promptly and unfailingly rewarded with the phrase "Atta good girl!" spoken in tones of rapture.

Twice a day after that, either Jack Humphrey or George Eustis escorted Morris and Buddy on a walk. From the chalet, they went down to the station from which the funicular railway descended the mountain to Vevey. There they worked over the route chosen for the day. Morris enjoyed it, but it was hard work both physically and mentally. The harness handle rubbed blisters on his hand. His left shoulder ached. The muscles of his calves and thighs stiffened.

There were a hundred things to remember. In addition to his daily walks, Morris had to give Buddy obedience exercises, brush and curry her, feed, water, and take her out to empty. He must do these things himself, so that Buddy would come to depend on him as he depended on her. When he fixed her food pan, he mixed the meat and meal with his bare hand so that Buddy would associate his scent with the pleasure of eating. If he forgot anything, Jack, George, or Dorothy were sure to catch him up.

As the end of a week, Jack announced that Morris was ready for a solo, a trip to Vevey and back without any comments, intervention, or help. "I'll be right behind you," Jack said, "but I'm not going to say a word unless you're in actual danger."

The walk to the funicular seemed strange without the usual commentary. Jack must be wearing rubber soles, because Morris could hear no footsteps. The sounds he could hear and even the feel of the road seemed unfamiliar. He thought he knew them so well. They should have reached the station long ago. Had he taken a wrong turn? Buddy stopped suddenly, and before Morris could check, he had stumbled up the concrete steps that led to the station.

Damn! His shins were bruised, but at least he knew where
he was.

In the cable car he sat down to feel his shins without
positioning Buddy out of the way under his knees as he
should have. She let out a yelp. Some son of a bitch had
stepped on her. Jack would give him hell for that.

In Vevey he forgot one turn and lost his way until the
tapping hammer in a cobbler's shop gave him a landmark.
Was Jack letting him get lost deliberately? He remembered
the rest of the route correctly, but stumbled at two curbs,
bumped a passerby, and forgot to reward Buddy half a
dozen times. He walked up the hill to Fortunate Fields
angry with Jack, himself, and the world.

"How did you make out?" Jack called from the chalet
entrance.

"You mean you weren't with me?"

Jack laughed. "Who do you think stepped on Buddy's
paw?"

Morris took a deep breath. "You son of a bitch!"

"Wasn't it a lovely day for a walk, Morris?" Dorothy
Eustis inquired sweetly. She was standing almost next to
him, but Morris recovered quickly.

"Oh, yes, madame," he agreed. "It was a lovely day."

One afternoon in Vevey, Jack directed Morris over a
strange route. When Buddy stopped for a curb, Morris
identified a down step with his cane, but Jack asked how
far down. Morris leaned forward and would have lost his
balance if Jack had not grabbed him around the waist.
Something was dragging at the cane. Water! Jack had ma-
neuvered him to the riverbank.

"Let that teach you never to step off a curb ahead of
your dog," Jack said.

Morris exploded, and this time Dorothy Eustis was not
there to interrupt. Jack waited until he was through, then
spoke seriously. "Look, boy. As long as you're here, you've
got me or George Eustis to look out for you. When you go

back to the States, there will be no one you can depend on but Buddy. I want to make damned sure you do."

Both during work and apart from it, Morris was feeling closer to Buddy every day. Currying her made him familiar with every curve of her beautiful body. At meals, he felt her head resting on his foot below the table. At night she slept up on the bed beside him, and her warm tongue licking his face woke him every morning. Before he left Vevey, two experiences completed his conversion to an almost religious faith in Buddy.

The first occurred on the sunken road leading up from the funicular to Fortunate Fields. Ahead of him and bearing down at a breakneck speed, he heard galloping hoofs and clattering wheels. For a brief instant, Buddy paused, then wheeled to the right and pulled him off the road up a steep embankment. Morris felt the harness handle rising nearly over his head, but he clung on tight and stumbled up after her. He reached the top only a moment before a pair of runaway horses dragging a heavy peasant cart thundered by. Jack Humphrey had seen it, but he had been too far behind Morris to come to the rescue. The quick-thinking and imperturable Buddy had done it all on her own.

The second experience was far less dramatic—even prosaic. Morris was sitting in the drawing room before lunch listening to Mrs. Eustis playing on one of the grand pianos.

"I need a haircut," he mused, fingering the hair above his ears. "Do you think Mr. Eustis could take me down to the barbershop this afternoon?"

The sounds of the piano paused. "You have Buddy, Morris," Mrs. Eustis suggested. "Why don't you go with her?"

Why didn't he go with her? The thought was staggering. It was long moments before he could take it in. He could go with Buddy. He didn't have to depend on a human guide, wait until it suited his convenience, and feel obligated for the favor afterward. He could go with Buddy, who would ask no thanks beyond the "Atta good girls" that were becoming second nature and who would feel proud and happy at the opportunity to work.

After lunch, Morris harnessed up Buddy and left for the funicular. In Vevey, he found his way to the barbershop and returned. The trip had none of the thrills of a narrow escape from runaway horses, and yet its meaning was far more exciting to Morris. A runaway team comes once in a lifetime. Haircuts come regularly every few weeks. Nothing could be more ordinary. And that is just the reason it is so hard to find a human guide to take a blind man for a haircut. Friends will be generous on important occasions, but it is the ordinary, prosaic little chores, the trips to the barbershop or post office, the purchase of shoelaces or toothpaste, that can be most frustrating by reason of their very simplicity.

Late that afternoon, sitting alone on the terrace overlooking the lake, Morris began to laugh. He couldn't stop. The more he tried, the harder he laughed. Mrs. Eustis overheard him and came out to find him alone, laughing as she had never heard him laugh before. "What in the world is the matter?" she asked.

It took Morris a moment to control himself. Then he explained.

"Back in Nashville, getting a haircut was a major event. Some days Father would drop me at the barbershop on his way to work and leave me there all morning until he could pick me up on his way home to lunch. Today, Buddy took me to get my hair cut. For the first time in four years, I'm free. That's why I was laughing. Because I'm free, by God, I'm free."

CHAPTER 4

Incorporation

MORRIS WAS made over. He was scarcely recognizable as the pale boy with hanging head and drooping shoulders who had stepped off the night train from Paris a month before. He walked with head erect, chest out, shoulders squared. In time, he would develop an almost military bearing. His voice rang with new confidence and his smile was radiant. He felt he had signed his personal Declaration of Independence, and he was eager to share his freedom with others.

Both Dorothy Eustis and Jack Humphrey were sympathetic. As a boy, Jack had had a younger brother, Leslie, born blind, and he had acted as Leslie's guide until his premature death. Dorothy had been reduced to tears by the cries of help she had received from blind Americans after publication of her _Post_ article. She would help Morris with advice and financial support, and they both agreed to help him find a trainer, but the school was his project. Their main interest was still in the program of Fortunate Fields. Its aim was scientific, not humanitarian. Its subject was dogs, not people. The idea of a guide dog school in the United States was Morris's alone. He named it after Dorothy's _Post_ article, The Seeing Eye.

They discussed Morris's plans with him. The first thing

he must do on his return was to test Buddy under American traffic conditions. He must expose her to the most congested areas of New York and any other large cities he passed through on his way to Nashville. He must prove that she was every bit as safe as a human guide and must demonstrate that fact to the American press and public. Once that had been accomplished, they would find him a trainer.

Morris and Buddy had a triumphant voyage home. Buddy was the hit of the Cunard liner *Tuscania* and was given free passage as a compliment to the work Morris planned. Once, after cashing a traveler's check with the purser, Morris returned to his cabin for a nap. He was just stretching out on his bunk when Buddy put up her paws and dropped something on his chest. It was his wallet. He had dropped it on the floor in the purser's office. Neither man had noticed, but Buddy had picked it up and carried it half the length of the ship back to the cabin.

On June 11 the *Tuscania* docked in New York. There Morris was met by Walter Wood and a crowd of reporters assigned to cover ship arrivals. Morris gave an interview in which the cockiness of his claims for Buddy got under one reporter's skin.

"You say that dog can take you anywhere?"

"Anywhere."

"Could she take you across West Street?"

"You show me to it, brother, and Buddy will cross it."

What Morris did not know was that West Street was popularly called "Death Street," and with good reason. Its vast cobblestone expanse churned with the horse-drawn and motor-driven traffic of the waterfront, unregulated by stoplights. Happy in his ignorance, Morris accompanied the reporter to the curb outside the dock entrance. When he had located the edge with his right foot, he gave Buddy the command of forward.

The next few minutes were among the longest in Morris's life. Clashing gears and roaring motors mingled with the clop of horses' hoofs and the whine of metal rims on cobblestones. Horns blew. Brakes squealed. Voices shouted. After Morris had taken only a few steps, Buddy backed violently to pull him away from a lumbering truck, then moved forward cautiously. Through the harness handle, he could feel her head jerking alertly from side to side, sizing up the situation. As she threaded this way and that, paused, backed, and moved forward again, Morris lost all sense of direction. For all he knew, they were describing a gigantic circle, but there was only one thing he could do: depend on Buddy. If he stepped out in front of her, if she lost her nerve or her judgment, their public failure would discredit his dream of a guide-dog school in America within an hour of their landing. But Buddy had nerves of steel and Morris had learned Jack's lesson at the river edge. Pulling Morris around a waiting taxi, Buddy signaled the opposite curb at last.

It was a magnificent feat. Nothing in Switzerland had prepared them for this. Yet Buddy had made the transition from the peaceful routine of shipboard life to the din and turmoil of Death Street without a qualm.

That evening after dinner, Morris put Buddy to the test on Broadway. As he later described it, "The theater hour was in full swing. Crowds were hurrying here and there on the sidewalk. Automobiles crowded the thoroughfares. But Buddy was as much at home in the seething mob as she had been on the quiet streets of Vevey. Not once did she falter, and not once did I bump into a soul."

He called on Robert Irwin at the American Foundation for the Blind. Irwin described the visit in his memoirs, contrasting it sharply with the call Morris had paid on his way to Vevey. Then, Irwin said, he had been "appalled by the terrors of New York traffic." On his return trip, Morris telephoned from the same hotel two miles away and made an appointment to come to the foundation an hour later. "Accompanied only by his dog, Frank traveled across the city on foot to the foundation offices and after a chat of an hour or so returned alone with his dog to his hotel." Morris

wrote Dorothy Eustis, "Mr. Irwin of the American Foundation wants a dog, so I need not say how my interview there
was."

At the ship, Walter had informed Morris that he was
to give a network radio speech the following evening, but
the talk was postponed, so Morris went to Washington,
where he met Paul McNutt and Frank Miller, who would
prove powerful allies in the federal bureaucracy in years
to come. On his return to New York, he found that his
radio speech had been postponed again. Since he had already
written it out, he gave the script to Walter to read and
started home to save the expense of staying in New York.

The radio speech began with a magniloquent reference
to the Declaration of Independence and its claim that all
men are created equal. The blind man, Morris said, was
excluded from his American birthright by his dependence
on family or friends to guide him on the most trivial errands.
"I have signed my Declaration of Independence and enjoy
it to the fullest with my dog Buddy."

The speech described Buddy's achievements during the
Broadway theater rush and went on to make two important
points. The first was that it is just as important for the
master to be trained in the use of his guide as for the dog
to be taught to guide. The second was that he planned to
open a nonprofit school, because he did not wish to see the
work falling into the hands of commercial breeders and
trainers as a moneymaking proposition.

Before Walter read this speech on the radio, Morris
had returned to Nashville, but on the way he stopped off
for a visit to his Aunt Selma in Cincinnati. Selma (Mrs.
Leo) Schwartz had been president of the National Council
of Jewish Women and was able to give Morris introductions
to leaders of the Jewish community throughout the United
States. This visit also gave him an opportunity to test Buddy
in downtown Cincinnati.

On June 20 he wrote the Eustises triumphantly. "I
am the happiest boy in all the world today, for I have gone

all over Nashville or, I should say, the business part of Nashville today visiting all my friends and having a marvelous feeling. . . . I have had two long distance calls, God knows how many letters, and how many people wanting to reserve dogs. It is like a stampede of people who have been locked up in a dark cell for many years rushing for the light." He was confident The Seeing Eye would be a big success. "Things are much easier than I anticipated."

A few days later, he wrote again, enclosing newspaper clippings. He proposed incorporating The Seeing Eye. *The New Outlook,* the publication of the American Foundation for the Blind, had asked for a 3,000-word article from him, and he was expecting to have a trolley-car pass for Buddy in a day or two.

Late in July, he received his first repsonse from Dorothy Eustis. She was totally absorbed in a course for communications dogs for the Swiss army, which had followed hard on the heels of a police course. Between the two, "George had managed to turn over the Rolls Royce, putting himself and two friends in the hospital." However, she assured Morris, "I think I have found just the man to handle the training for you."

By the time Morris received this letter, he had had inquiries from blind people in all forty-eight states and had been offered enough dogs "to run my school for a year. For the first fifty dogs, I shall not have to go out of my state. I have also been promised a lot in a convenient location, enough lumber to build my kennels with and wire offered me at cost. . . . I believe within one year or two, when our school is firmly established, we will be able to turn over a small endowment to the American Foundation for the Blind, that they will add quite a sum to it and make The Seeing Eye a permanent organization. Mr. Irwin was quite enthusiastic over this idea."

On his side, Morris felt he had everything ready to go. He had the blind applicants, the dogs, the kennel, and the potential backing of the American Foundation. He needed only the trainer Dorothy Eustis and Jack Humphrey had promised him. He could not have anticipated that this would prove a very difficult problem and that he would not hear from Mrs. Eustis for nearly two months.

Gretchen Green's picture of life at Mt. Pèlerin in the summer of 1928 might suggest that Dorothy was simply too busy to attend to Morris's problems.

> A course of liaison dogs is in training with Dorothy Eustis doing the actual training herself. Fortunate Fields is under military discipline. No one is allowed to enter during working hours without permission. Mrs. Theodore Roosevelt telephoned from Lausanne to ask if she might come up with Ethel and her children. She did come—staunch exquisite little lady, standing hours to watch dogs and men.
>
> It is fun running according to schedule. A bugle sounds reveille at six. Breakfast follows, and obedience exercises (the latter for dogs, not guests), then training throughout the day, and sometimes during the night. The dogs will be the communications for the army, carrying telephone wires, messages in tin capsules, and carrier pigeons in baskets on their backs.
>
> In need of a hostile force, the household is drafted, the guests enlisting for vanguard. Some days there are forced marches three miles over the mountains. A cart equipped with food drives on before, the hostile force following in the rear. The heat is terrific. Army and foe bivouac at noon under the trees, fortifying themselves with goat cheese and milk. Night raids are startling. As the dogs run between trenches, the enemy hurls giant crackers for bombs, all to accustom them to the gentle art of war. Dorothy, dogs and soldiers train for six weeks and set out for maneuvers tomorrow.

But Dorothy's preoccupation with the liaison course was not the reason for the delay in sending Morris a trainer. Dorothy and Jack had been overconfident about the ease of procuring a German trainer. Those working for the government had liberal pension benefits which they would have to forfeit if they went to the United States. The compensation they asked in return made them too expensive.

There were a few trainers who were not employed by the government, but selecting one was not easy. Dorothy's first choice, Herr Stiersdorfer, had fractured his skull in the accident with George Eustis. Herr Knapp was considered seriously, but she decided he lacked initiative.

Another cause for delay was the disruption of her private life. Dorothy had become increasingly aware of her basic incompatibility with her husband. The accident with the car had been the last straw. He had been driving too fast because he had not left enough time to catch a train. It was careless. Worse, it was stupid. She hated to give up on anything, but she had to admit this marriage was a failure. They were hopelessly mismatched. Having made up her mind, she did not hesitate. She started divorce proceedings while George was still in the hospital.

Dorothy later tended to minimize George Eustis's contribution to Fortunate Fields, because he lacked her deep interest and commitment. Jack Humphrey was more generous. He said of George that "in the early stages, he was a great help due to his facility with various languages and a natural training ability. He worked equally with me on the first two dogs, Kiss and Gala, and worked equally with me on teaching Morris to work with Buddy." Although George Eustis's contribution to The Seeing Eye was very brief, it was real, and his talents were missed. If the marriage had lasted another year, it is at least conceivable that George could have come to the United States to train the first class or two.

As the summer wore to a close and Dorothy returned from successful maneuvers with the dogs, her thoughts again turned to Stiersdorfer. She wrote to Morris, "Thanks to his good health and habits, he is well on the road to recovery. I am going to Karlsruhe to see the dogs he has trained there. If everything meets with my approval he is ready to come in January."

Meanwhile, Morris, still ignorant of the pending divorce, was firing off one letter after another. He had investigated the immigration quota. It would be no problem for a trainer, since he could remain in America five years on a visa. He was ready to select his board and apply for a charter, but he received no answers to his letters, and his anxiety mounted.

On October 15, he wrote, "My dear Mr. and Mrs. Eustis. Since it has been five weeks since I have received any communication from you, I am forced to stop work on The Seeing Eye." He could go no further without information on the raising of the money, the choice of a trainer, the number of dogs he could train per month, his salary, and place of origin. He went on to describe his problems. Americans are afraid of shepherds and seem to consider Buddy "a wild lion." Even those who accept Buddy at face value express doubts that dogs like her could be put out in numbers. "Oh, if I only had you here to sit down and talk these things over quickly! The slow mails cramp my style of work."

Within a few days, Morris had a clarifying letter. "Yesterday I was granted my divorce from Mr. Eustis which I expect explains a number of things to you." She was optimistic about Stiersdorfer. Mr. Humphrey had looked over the dogs he trained at Karlsruhe, and they seemed sound, but she wanted Stiersdorfer to go to Potsdam with Humphrey for three weeks. Then she wanted him to spend a month or so at Fortunate Fields, so that she could be absolutely sure of his work. In the same letter, she gave Morris some personal advice that would be repeated often. "You must educate the public to the fact that Buddy is a working instrument first and a dog second. No one should pat her or touch her. It will double the difficulty of the work she has to do." With a tart humor that occasionally spiced her letters, she appealed to his "common sense (of which, every now and then, I get a glimpse!!!)."

She promised Morris that she would come to Nashville in January, but even as he was reading this good news, she was having misgivings about Stiersdorfer. There was something about him she did not trust. Her mind turned to another possibility.

In June, her ward Esther Rowland had been married to Henry Clifford at Fortunate Fields. One member of the wedding party had been Henry's younger sister, Adelaide. At eighteen, Adelaide Clifford was a handsome, talented, and athletic girl more than ordinarily uncertain as to what to do with her life. Her father had died soon after she was born. Subsequently, her mother had remarried, but the marriage had ended in divorce. Adelaide had spent five years in a Swiss boarding school at Montreux before returning to the States to graduate from finishing school. Now, except for a passionate attachment to the family summer place in Maine, she lacked emotional roots.

She had meant to spend only a few days at Fortunate Fields, but she felt at home in French Switzerland, and she was fascinated by the work of the dogs. Under Jack Humphrey's tutelage, she was soon helping with the training and proved to have real talent for it. It was far more exciting than the life of a New York debutante, and in addition to Jack, Nettie Humphrey encouraged her to take it seriously.

Nearly fifty years later, Adelaide recalled, "I got into pants and big boots and loved it. Hell! I was the first hippie."

She had been working with guide dogs for months now and could work a dog blindfold around Vevey. Dorothy asked Jack whether Adelaide could be trusted as trainer for The Seeing Eye in Nashville. Jack said that she had trained dogs all right, but had yet to train a blind person. Until she had, she would need the supervision of someone more experienced.

Dorothy pondered. Morris had blind students lined up

and waiting. Nearly six months ago, she had promised him that she would find him a trainer, and she had not made good on her promise. Reluctantly, she came to a decision. She told Jack that he must go to Nashville with Adelaide to train the first class.

Jack hit the ceiling. He had come to Switzerland for scientific research. Four long years of selective breeding, thorough training, and painstaking analysis were just beginning to produce data with potential significance for the whole field of genetics. Now she was asking him to interrupt his research and leave his wife and son for months to help a harebrained college kid in Nashville.

Both Jack and Dorothy had steel wills, and neither was accustomed to take orders. Their contract wisely took their characters into account. It provided that, in case of a conflict, each of them would hold their peace for two weeks. If they still felt like it at the end of that time, they could dissolve the partnership. Jack steamed in silence for fourteen days, then wrote out his resignation and placed it on the tray that would be carried up to Mrs. Eustis with her breakfast next morning.

But as Woollcott wrote years later in *The New Yorker,* "Mrs. Eustis never got that letter. For in the hour before dawn, Humphrey, waking from a troubled sleep, sneaked down, and tore it up. . . . For the first time in years, he had dreamed of his brother Leslie. He had heard the remembered little voice calling to him as it always used to do— calling to him for help." The years since he had run away from home in his teens had been so eventful that Humphrey's memories of his childhood in Saratoga Springs were buried deep, but little Leslie had been an important part of that distant world. Jack had been his constant guide, had even taken him along to school, so that he could look out for him during classes. Leslie's death had lifted a heavy burden of responsibility from young Jack, but it had also left a permanent sorrow slumbering far below the hardboiled exterior of the grown man.

And so once again the development of The Seeing Eye was rescued by coincidence, the coincidence that the self-taught genius who managed Fortunate Fields just happened to have had a younger blind brother. Jack could refuse to obey the orders of Dorothy Eustis, but he could not resist the voice of Leslie. He agreed to go to Nashville.

Dorothy wrote Morris, "So as not to disappoint you, I am disrupting my whole organization and sending you Jack Humphrey for two or three months to get things established and organized and to train the first batch of dogs for you. He will bring over at least three trained dogs. And I hope to send to Nashville with him an assistant trainer, Miss Adelaide Clifford, who has been working with me for the last three months and is a natural born trainer."

Morris was ecstatic. "Mr. Humphrey is just the man to get The Seeing Eye rolling. With his personality there will be no trouble."

Dorothy assigned Morris a number of tasks. She wanted kennels ready for eight dogs as near the route they were to work as possible. This route should take about forty minutes, and Morris should plan to have it include busy streets, trolley cars, and crossings, both the kind controlled by policemen and those controlled only by lights. If people were to come from out of town, they would need a place to stay. Also, there should be a meeting room near the kennels where the class could listen to Mr. Humphrey's lectures, rest after work, and study braille maps of the route.

She was having a Fortunate Fields dog trained for Dr. Howard Buchanan in the first class. A second Fortunate Fields dog was very beautiful and should go to "as well-to-do a person as possible." A third and possibly a fourth dog "will not be of our breeding and therefore more ordinary. I tell you this so you can fit the people to them." The implication is that ordinary dogs are for ordinary people. Beautiful dogs are for the well-to-do, who are not ordinary.

She expected to get the third and fourth dogs from Potsdam, where Jack had gone "for a three weeks' brushup and will at the same time study the question of a trainer to take his place when he comes back, but you don't have to worry about that part of the question, you lucky dog!!!"

Morris answered, "I may be a lucky dog not having to find a trainer, but this preparing things over here is nobody's joke." He enumerated his difficulties. Then, with considerable pride, he outlined the people he had selected for his board. Before Dorothy could receive his letter, she wrote to ask about this board and expressed her concern that it be representative. Huger Jervey, Dean of the Columbia Law School, who had been staying at Fortunate Fields, had given her letters to some important people in Memphis and Nashville. She suggested that since Miss Adelaide Clifford was a member of the Junior League, the Nashville chapter might be involved. She referred to her forthcoming trip, saying that since most of her time would be devoted to fund raising in New York and Philadelphia, she would stay in Nashville only three days. "Much as I would like to stop with you and your mother, I think it would really be better to be put up at some hotel. I will have so many people to see and so many calls to make that I think it would be best." Of a banquet Morris proposed, she wrote, "If the banquet is a Dutch treat, I'll come with pleasure, but I'd hate like fury to have it given at the expense of friends of The Seeing Eye."

Morris replied politely, but under the surface we feel him bristling at what he takes to be Mrs. Eustis's condescending attitude. So she has letters to some important people in Nashville, does she! Does she think he doesn't know any important people in Nashville?

"My board, with no credit to myself, is one of the most representative that could be formed in this part of the country: Governor and Mrs. Horton, Mr. Roger S. Caldwell, one of the South's biggest financiers, Mr. Lee J. Loventhal, one of the biggest social workers in the city, Chancellor Kirkland of Vanderbilt University, Dr. Payne of Peabody College for Teachers, Mr. J. P. W. Brown, head of the local railroad and light company, Mr. C. A. Craig, president of the largest life insurance company in the South," and so forth. The Nashville chapter of the Junior League was too much involved with crippled children to be of any assistance, but Frances Dudley Brown, national president of the Junior League, was a neighbor and had agreed to serve on the board.

"Of course, you do what is convenient for you, although I believe you will find it most convenient to stay at my home, as it is quiet and only fifteen minutes from the city. You will have a private bedroom, bath, and sitting room. Miss Freeman, my mother's secretary, aids her in looking after the house. . . . A car will be at your disposal the entire time you are in the city. . . . We have decided not to have a banquet, but instead have a buffet supper. . . . My mother and father will do this in your honor." It would cost The Seeing Eye nothing. He might have liked to add, "We know how to do things too, even if we weren't born on the Main Line."

But having vented his pique, he closed with a rush of enthusiasm. "I am much more excited over your coming than I was over my going to Europe." Differences in their age, temperament, and background would continue to be sources of friction between Morris and Dorothy Eustis throughout their association, but these always melted away in the ardor of their common devotion to the guide-dog movement.

Yet there was a difference in their perspective even here. The American Seeing Eye filled Morris's whole horizon. He expressed his commitment to it in religious terms. "This work shall not fail, and by the God that made me, I shall leave no stone unturned until The Seeing Eye is on a firm running basis." Dorothy Eustis was behind the American school foursquare. She was sending over Jack Humphrey and she promised financial backing, but she saw America as only part of the picture. If Morris was right, in a year or two The Seeing Eye would be taken over as a division of the American Foundation. Her contribution to the guide-dog movement should be international.

Already, she had conceived the idea of an international training school for guide-dog instructors. It would require considerable resources. At least in the beginning, Fortunate Fields could supply the dogs, but the school would also need apprentice instructors, their blind students, and a building in which to house instructors, students, and dogs. Dorothy could not afford to underwrite the entire project herself. But Gretchen Green had a friend who might help—she always did—and she invited Marjorie Chadbourne, just then in Paris, to come for a visit. She stayed for some days and seemed much interested in watching Adelaide Clifford and Jack Humphrey working the dogs, but left without making any commitment. Not long afterward, there was a visit from Huger Jervey. Marjorie Chadbourne had asked his advice on the project, and when he approved, she agreed to back it. An international school was planned under the name L'Oeil Qui Voit. With the exception of Jack Humphrey's salary, it was to be underwritten entirely by Mrs. Chadbourne.

When Dorothy, Gretchen, Adelaide, and two Fortunate Fields dogs sailed for New York in December 1928, the newspapers covered the story. Adelaide, described as "having deserted the ranks of society for the equally exhausting life of dog trainer," was quoted on plans for an international school. It would be directed by Captain George Balsiger, who had worked with Mrs. Eustis on the liaison course that summer. A cavalry veterinarian, he had agreed to rent his house and kennels in Lausanne for school headquarters. Thus, even as she steamed toward America, Dorothy was planning for a Seeing Eye on the other side of the Atlantic.

It had been settled that Jack would precede her to Nashville. She would arrive on January 5. Gretchen Green had scheduled her for speaking dates or dinners, including appearances at the New York Lighthouse, the Colony Club, and the Cosmopolitan Club, on January 2, 12, 15, 16, and 18. She would sail for Europe on January 19.

The results of Dorothy's whirlwind visit to Nashville were summed up in a memorandum she prepared the day before she sailed. It reported that she had raised a sum of $7,500 to cover the 1929 budget. Of this, $3,500 was for administration, including a salary of $1,500 for Morris as managing director, a secretary, office equipment, and incidental expenses. Morris was to recruit blind people who wanted guide dogs. He would also administer a revolving fund of $4,500 to underwrite the purchase and training of the dogs. The fund was to be renewed with the money paid by blind students who could afford it or with scholarships contributed by individuals or groups.

Mrs. Eustis's visit was a social success as well. The buffet at the Franks' was festive, and the motion pictures of the training at Vevey were greeted enthusiastically. As balm to Morris's ego, the Philadelphia blue blood who had tried to evade his invitation wrote, "Will you please thank your mother for her charming hospitality and tell her that I have never stayed in a household so cheerful and sunny as hers."

On January 29, 1929, The Seeing Eye was issued its certificate of incorporation. On February 1, Morris reported to Mrs. Eustis that he had rented an office in the Fourth and First National Bank Building for fifteen dollars a month and had bought a typewriter desk, a plain desk, four chairs, and a coat tree for another fifteen. "How's that for putting the Scotch trick on them?"

His jubilation is understandable. He was managing director of The Seeing Eye, Incorporated, with a board, a budget, an office, a trainer, and, best of all, a class about to begin. But the woman who had made all this possible was back in Switzerland preparing to give a two-month course to Mussolini's police in Rome. She and Morris would not meet face-to-face for nearly a year, and The Seeing Eye would undergo many vicissitudes in the interim.

BOOK II

Nomadic Adolescence

CHAPTER 5

The Nashville Classes

ON HIS way to Nashville from Fortunate Fields, Jack Humphrey stopped off for a few days to visit his friends Willi and Florence Ebeling at Lake Openaka in Dover, New Jersey. Willi had met Jack five years before in Boston, where he had heard Jack lecture on the breeding of German shepherds. They had been drawn to each other from the start. The Ebelings were breeders of shepherds with a keen appreciation of their working qualities. They were acquainted with Dorothy Eustis and had been following the progress of the Fortunate Fields experiment with the greatest interest.

Willi was then forty-six, slight of stature, nattily attired, with piercing gray eyes and a quizzical smile habitually playing around the corners of his mouth. He had been born Willi Heinrich Karl Louis Ebeling in a tiny German village not far from Bremen. He came to America as the representative of a Bremen firm of importers in 1904. Three years later he became engaged to Florence Evans, the daughter of an American importer, and they were married in 1908. After World War I, Ebeling retired from his own prosperous firm to become a gentleman farmer at Lake Openaka. The house overlooking their spacious private lake had originally been a swimming club, which the Ebelings adapted to their own uses. When the difficulty of getting help made farming impractical, they converted their former hen house into kennels and began breeding German shepherds.

Willi Ebeling delighted in good conversation, and over billiards or sipping brandy in the darkly paneled living room, Jack regaled him with stories of the work at Fortunate Fields. Before he was through, Jack had so fired Willi with enthusiasm that he volunteered to come to Nashville at his own expense to take instruction in guide-dog technique from Jack. The Ebelings had no children, and although Willi was about to become editor of *Shepherd Dog Review*, he was unencumbered and "ready for a lark." He little suspected that it would lead to a second career, more challenging than the first.

Through Willi, Jack first heard of Josef Weber, the German who had opened a training kennel outside Princeton. Weber had trained dogs for the Berlin police and was familiar with the guide-dog work at Potsdam. Willi and Jack drove over in Willi's seven-passenger Packard to meet him. At Jack's suggestion, Weber agreed to come to Nashville to learn Jack's modifications of the Potsdam technique. The Seeing Eye would pay his expenses, and it was understood that, if all went well, Weber would contract to train dogs for the school. Since Adelaide was also coming to Nashville, Jack hoped that by the time he returned to Switzerland, he would leave behind three people schooled in the basics of guide-dog instruction. Jack went ahead to Nashville to look over "the kennels of which Mr. Frank had written" and to pick over the dogs of which he had boasted. To his disgust, he found there were no kennels outside Morris's imagination and that all the dogs were puppies, too young for training. With his customary energy, he found an old building to rent and had it equipped with fencing and stalls for the dogs. Combing Nashville and its environs, he could find only three dogs, and two of them were of uncertain temperament. He turned to Willi Ebeling, who arranged a shipment of six bitches of his own breeding. A seventh came from a woman in Wellesley, Massachusetts. One of the Ebeling dogs was questionable, but Jack, ever alert to turn a problem to his advantage, kept the three uncertain dogs to illustrate to his apprentices what made them undesirable.

Weber was unable to leave Princeton until late February, but Adelaide and Willi Ebeling showed up promptly. Jack assigned Adelaide three dogs to train on her own. This enabled him to devote his full time to Willi Ebeling. The teenaged girl in pants and boots, the bowlegged cowboy with snuff under his lip, and the retired importer in voluminous plus fours and argyle stockings were soon a familiar sight working with their shepherds on the streets of Nashville.

By February 2, Jack had tuned up Gala and Tartar for the two students of the first American class. It is worth emphasizing that Jack had trained these dogs personally at Fortunate Fields. Letters from representatives of the Potsdam school to Robert Irwin and the Shepherd Dog Club of America claimed he had not. When Mrs. Eustis had asked permission for Humphrey to spend three weeks in Potsdam, they said they had suspected her commercial motives and had therefore allowed Humphrey to see only dogs that were already fully trained, so that he would be able to learn nothing. Later, when she had asked to buy two trained dogs for America, "We refused categorically Mrs. E.'s demand. Unfortunately, Mrs. E. succeeded to get two trained dogs from another school of training and took them with her. These dogs were never trained by Mr. H. himself."

This was nonsense. Assisted by George Eustis, Jack had trained Gala nearly a year before at Fortunate Fields. She had been intended for Dr. Buchanan of Monmouth, Illinois, and though he had had to cancel his trip to Switzerland, she was paired with him now in Nashville. Tartar was another beautiful Fortunate Fields dog. Mrs. Eustis had recommended that she be paired with "as well-to-do a person as possible," and Morris had chosen another doctor, R. V. Harris of Savannah, Georgia. Both doctors were active, intelligent men in their middle years, and the class began well. Morris's chief worry was not with their work, but with their lodgings, "because we could not get rooms for them anywhere near the kennel." Buchanan was staying at the Y.M.C.A. and the more affluent Harris at the Andrew Jackson Hotel.

"It is not at all satisfactory for either students, dogs, or trainers." Morris wrote Dorothy. "There are at least twenty-four boarding houses within a few blocks, but after personally calling on them, I was all but thrown out as soon as I told them I wanted a place for two blind men and their dogs. Therefore, The Seeing Eye will be forced to either rent or buy a house."

This was typical of Morris's impetuous logic. He went on to describe a house for which he recommended a year's lease with option to buy and the expenditure of about a thousand dollars in furnishings and improvements, "even though it will be vacant for nine months." He had consulted neither Jack Humphrey nor Willi Ebeling on this scheme, and Dorothy Eustis's response was predictably cool. She reminded Morris that The Seeing Eye was still in an experimental stage. She did not want to spend money "until we see what we are doing. You want to gauge what there is to do next year in a factual way before launching yourself high and wide."

But Morris's mood continued high and wide. In the growing confidence and enthusiasm of doctors Buchanan and Harris, he relived the excitement of his own emancipation with Buddy, and he shared fully in the triumph of their graduation. It would be proof to the skeptics that Buddy was not an isolated phenomenon and that The Seeing Eye could turn out competent guides in numbers. His optimism was buttressed by a letter from Buchanan, written from home. "Gala is doing fine. I go everywhere alone, getting into places I want, sometimes with a little trouble, but generally without trouble and always get home safe and thankful to God that I did it without having to ask some member of my family or friend to go with me. I do not have to stay at home now, because I hate to ask my wife to stop her work or daughter to stop her play to go with me."

Meanwhile, preparations for the second class were going forward. Morris wrote Dorothy, "Mr. Weber came Saturday night and I liked him very much. The rest of the gang are grumbling about our weather, snow fifteen inches deep, the first in eleven years. Jack Humphrey is out of snuff and can't get the same brand in town, so you can imagine what a pleasant lunch we had today." Two weeks later he announced that he had lined up seven students for the March 28 class, five of them from Nashville, three paid for by scholarships. The biggest news was that he had arranged to have Adelaide Clifford turn over a dog to Herbert Immeln in New York in May.

Herbert Immeln was the highly respected director of the Lighthouse, which had been founded as the New York Association for the Blind in 1905. The Lighthouse was well endowed, and although it was not a national organization, it performed all the functions of the New York State Commission for the Blind within the city. In addition, it operated a varied assortment of recreational, social, cultural, and artistic programs. Dorothy Eustis had spoken at the Lighthouse in the preceding January, shortly before her departure for Europe, and apparently her remarks had been sufficiently persuasive to cause Immeln to visit Nashville to see for himself. His decision to apply for a dog constituted an important breakthrough in the wall of prejudice among workers for the blind. Both Morris and Dorothy had been delighted to learn of Edward Allen's announcement the previous January: "I am a convert to the modern guidance of man by a dog, because it is so totally different from the ancient and medieval way." But if Allen's word carried weight, Immeln's example would be far more telling.

Curiously, Dorothy did not even refer to Immeln in her reply to Morris. Perhaps she was skeptical. She advised Morris not to invest too much of himself in the job of managing director since it was "a work that will never take up a man's whole time." In any case, the executive committee in Nashville confirmed arrangements for two future classes. Adelaide Clifford would be paid fifty dollars each for turning over dogs to Immeln and a Mr. Hendrick of Norfolk, Virginia, in May. Weber would be paid $170 each for both training and turning over three dogs in New York City in July. Adelaide would be brought down from Maine at Seeing Eye expense to pass on the safety of Weber's dogs before the end of the class.

Meanwhile, although one of the Nashville students had dropped out at the last moment, the March 28 class had gotten off to a spirited start, thanks to a telegram from Dr. Harris. It read in part: "You are about to start the most enjoyable journey of your darkness. My experience assures you that you may place implicit confidence in your instuctors and confidence and faith in your dogs. Life's pathway is strewn with many pitfalls and dangers, but your dog will successfully negotiate for you all of these and protect you at all times. Let your watchwords be Courage and Perseverance. Thank God, the Great Master, for The Seeing Eye and your instructors."

Four of the six students were from Nashville: E. A. Rogers, Sidney Sweeney, Mac Alexander, and Earl Pendleton. Young Pendleton was in his last year at the Tennessee School for the Blind, and because authorities there were anxious about a dog's behavior in the crowded corridors, dining hall, and classrooms, his application was approved only after considerable discussion. The two remaining students were from out of state: Mrs. Elford Eddy of Berkeley, California, the first woman student, and Dr. R. A. Blair, a clergyman from Parnassus, Pennsylvania. Three years earlier he had been a missionary in China when his retina detached.

Blair's letter of inquiry to Morris showed he was exactly the sort of man The Seeing Eye wanted. It was utterly devoid of self-pity. "I can read braille," he explained, "and write on the typewriter as I am doing now, but I cannot visit my flock. My wife who took me on calls at first is now an invalid, bedridden for a year and a half. My daughter is a cripple with infantile paralysis, so cannot help me to get around. If I had a dog to take me about the parish, that would overcome about the only handicap I now suffer from blindness." But when faced with the reality of working a dog in a strange city, the confidence and courage reflected in this letter deserted Blair. In his nervous agitation and confusion, he was forever giving the wrong commands and pulling against his dog instead of following her. By the end of a week, she was so bewildered by his incomprehensible behavior that she refused to work for him at all.

E. A. Rogers with Pal, Sidney Sweeney with Anitra, and Earl Pendleton with Muddles were all coming along nicely, but Alexander was proving a problem. He was sixty-three years old, feeble, and so rheumatic that he ought never to have been admitted to a class. If his Dot moved with any haste, as she would surely have to do at times working in traffic, he lost his balance. After a week, Jack Humphrey decided that he would never make part of a safe man-dog unit and dropped him from the class. This enabled him to substitute Dot for the dog Dr. Blair had spoiled and to give the clergyman a second chance.

Mrs. Eddy posed a different sort of problem. Her husband had accompanied her on the long train trip from California, and his constant presence both in the hotel and on the street confused her dog, Beda. She seemed uncertain as to which of the Eddys was her master. Mr. Eddy was also a distraction to his wife. Aware of his presence as a potential protector from harm, Mrs. Eddy unconsciously withheld full confidence in her instructor, Willi Ebeling, and even more important, in Beda.

Jack and Willi discussed the situation. Jack took Mr.

Eddy aside, and Willi Ebeling directed Mrs. Eddy and Beda down a congested street without her husband hovering in the background. Later she recalled it as the crucial moment in her adjustment. As she was following Beda through the crowd, she heard Willi Ebeling calling to her to stop. She obeyed, and he came up breathless with excitement to inform her that Beda had just taken her around an open manhole. "Mr. Ebeling's excitment was contagious, and my heart started to pound. That incident established my confidence in the dog and The Seeing Eye and engendered an everlasting devotion to Mr. Ebeling."

The moment may have been equally crucial for Ebeling. The retired importer had come to Nashville on a lark, but the work engrossed his interest increasingly day by day. Under Jack's instruction, he had taught guide work to Beda, a dog of his own breeding. Taking and passing a blindfold test with her had been a tremendous thrill, but still it had been a game. He had watched with alarm the consequences of Mrs. Eddy's failure to place full faith in Beda. By some canine power of intuition, she sensed that part of her mistress was hanging back. Then had come this moment, a sudden fusing of woman and dog into a smoothly functioning unit, as Beda guided her around the yawning manhole. This was no game. This was reality of the highest order, a miracle for which he could take no credit, but for which he had served as a sort of catalyst. It was a moment of supreme excitement, and he had called out to Mrs. Eddy to share it with her.

In the meanwhile, under the tutelage of Herr Weber, Blair was beginning to acquire confidence in Dot and he, too, had a revelation. It happened on a morning when Weber lost a trouser button midway on the route. There was a tailor shop across the street, and Weber told Blair to wait while he had the button sewed on. While Weber was in the shop, the foreman of a demolition crew spoke to Blair. He was about to set off a charge of dynamite, he said, and asked Blair to move down to the end of the block.

Inside the shop where he had given his pants to the tailor, Weber saw Blair and Dot moving off. He rushed into the street in his shorts, yelling to Blair to stop. The minister was hugely delighted by the episode, which somehow demonstrated that he and Dot had a joint independent existence apart from their instructor. It was the turning point in his training.

On his return to Parnassaus, he wrote Morris: "Dot and I go out walking every morning and walk between fifteen and seventeen blocks, and then go calling in the afternoon and evening. She took me to church Sabbath morning and lay at my feet in the pulpit while I preached."

Mrs. Eddy was the last member of the class to graduate, and Jack Humphrey accompanied the Eddys to the railroad station to see them off. While Mr. Eddy took Beda to the baggage car, Mrs. Eddy tried to express her gratitude to Jack. He cut her off with a grunt. She began again, but as she was still speaking, he turned and walked away without uttering a word.

At that moment, Mr. Eddy returned from the baggage car, and she described Humphrey's discourtesy. Mr. Eddy, who had seen Jack leave, told her he couldn't talk.

"Why not?" she wanted to know.

"Well, you see, my dear, he was crying."

CHAPTER 6

Wawasee
and Astoria

FOR THE first four months of 1929, Seeing Eye activities had been centered in Nashville, but the climate was much too hot for year-round training, and after the second class there was a general exodus. Weber returned to Princeton, and Willi Ebeling to Openaka. Before departing for Switzerland, Jack spent a few days with the Ebelings. Adelaide, too, moved into Openaka to put the finishing touches on Bella and Betty for her May class. From his office in Nashville, the managing director reported that things were mighty quiet.

Adelaide wrote him, "We all took Jack to the boat last Friday, and, believe me, I was never so sorry to see anybody go before. It almost feels as if the bottom of everything had dropped out." But she was soon driving her dogs into nearby Morristown for work, and she wrote to Morris, "Saw Weber yesterday. He has got three dandy dogs to train. Willi and I tested them out for temperament."

Willi Ebeling was beginning to play an important role. In the absence of Jack Humphrey, he was authorized to pass on the safety of man-dog units before they were graduated. This was a crucial function and one no blind man could perform. He also undertook the acquisition of dogs suitable for guide work. His own stock, his knowledge of fellow breeders, his editorship of *Shepherd Dog Review*, and his work in Nashville qualified him uniquely for this job. Finally, Dorothy Eustis and Jack Humphrey counted on him to advise Morris on business matters. The effect was to divide power and authority between Nashville, Openaka, and Mt. Pelerin, and the inevitable result was tension.

Some of the irritants were petty. Morris's custody of the equipment in Nashville was awkward, especially since most of it had come originally from Switzerland. Before the May 9 class, Morris sent Adelaide two harnesses, leashes, muzzles, currycombs, and brushes, but only one feed pan. "Why you didn't send two feed pans is beyond me!" she protested, while Willi Ebeling told Morris the muzzles he sent were entirely too large; he had bought proper ones and was sending the others back. Later Adelaide returned some leashes: "For crying out loud, the next time you get leashes, get good ones like ours."

Expense accounts were another source of friction. Adelaide felt Morris's payments were grudging, and accompanied her accounting with the assurance, "I have only spent what was absolutely necessary." During the class she would live with her mother in Manhattan. Immeln lived in Astoria. "The first week we shall work in Astoria, as it is quieter for the beginning. Therefore, I shall have to spend carfare between my house and Astoria. I take it for granted you will pay my expenses. Am I right?" Since she had to ask, she could not really have taken it for granted, and there is something absurd about a New York debutante haggling with The Seeing Eye's managing director over carfare.

Willi Ebeling's letters could also be trivial. The laundry in Nashville had shrunk a prize pair of his golf stockings, and several exchanges dealt with Morris's futile attempts to have them brought up to size. Occasionally, Willi was astringent. If he had not already done so, he hoped Morris would write letters of thanks to Jack, Adelaide, and Mrs.

Eustis and make sure "that the nice things you will say are not spoiled by the 'customary little dirty digs.' "

Elsewhere Willi dwelt on fundamental differences of opinion. When they were in Nashville together, Morris had wired Charles Campbell and Edward Van Cleve for advice. From his standpoint this was perfectly natural. The Seeing Eye was an agency for the blind, and he was consulting the heads of other agencies for the blind who were known to his mother. But to Jack and Willi, the opinions of workers for the blind had no bearing on Seeing Eye affairs, where a knowledge of dogs was what mattered. Campbell, Van Cleve, and the rest knew nothing about dogs, and their opinions were therefore worthless.

Willi wrote, "You still seem to have a habit of asking opinions. Stop asking opinions. Work to turn out a product that is so good that it will form the opinion, and then you will know that the opinion of the world is with you. I thought we drove that lesson home to you when we were in Nashville."

He said Morris had missed the chance of a lifetime by not having Jack Humphrey talk to the Nashville Lions Club. Morris promptly went before the Lions himself. He reported triumphantly that the Nashville chapter would propose a resolution to the International Lions meeting in Louisville on June 18. It would ask "that the work of The Seeing Eye be adopted in the program of work for the blind by every chapter in the United States and that they lend their support and cooperation by forming classes and giving scholarships."

He sent Willi Ebeling the draft of a pamphlet he wished to take to Louisville and asked for revisions. Willi made a number of improvements, and Morris acknowledged that "all corrections are splendid." Willi Ebeling's feeling for the precise meaning and nuance of language was to prove invaluable.

Meanwhile, Adelaide had started her adjustment of

Immeln and Hedrick with Bella and Betty. "Immeln is doing a great piece of work with his dog, and everything is tic-tac, so I am very pleased." Hedrick was showing improvement but "is the clumsiest fellow I ever saw, forever stepping on the bitch."

A few days later, "Immeln is doing now what he should be doing in his third week, he is so far advanced. Bella, although in heat, is working tic-tac with him, and you would think they had been working for five years together. He has a broad grin on his face when he is working. His only fear appears to be the elevated trains overhead, which deafen him when crossing the street. This, however, has been good practice for him, as he has had to depend on his dog. Bella is a changed girl. She took him over in two or three days. She is in perfect condition with the slickest coat you ever saw. I understand from Mrs. Immeln that Immeln spends half an hour every morning cleaning her, and at night Mrs. Immeln says the two are so slushy she can hardly sit in the same room with them."

Hedrick, too, was working much better. His main fault was failure to reward his dog "in a laughing enough manner." He managed to graduate and went home with Betty to Norfolk, but Immeln was the real star.

On May 30, "We took Immeln down to Forty-Second Street and Fifth Avenue to work his dog in front of the president of the New York Association for the Blind and the Police Commissioner, who directed traffic for twenty minutes. There were a lot of reporters and people to take pictures." Willi Ebeling exulted, "Immeln is the brightest star we have hit to this day." Fox Movietone took talking pictures with Immeln speaking, "which will be shown all over the world."

This was news Morris sorely needed. He had just received a letter from Dorothy Eustis that raked him over the coals for a number of lapses in both his letters and his administration of Seeing Eye affairs. "You are not accurate either in your work or in your statements, and in each case it brings discredit on The Seeing Eye. . . . You do not weigh conditions, and therefore you come to your conclusions unsupported by facts or reason. . . . Your secretary is careless in her typing. Your administrative work is under inspection because of your amateur methods. Your excuse, that you are young, is no reason for not learning by experience. As I have told you, it is pardonable to make a mistake the first time, but to make it again is just plain dumb. Your indiscriminate use of telegrams with their attendant expense is deplorable. You need to temper your statements with facts and remember always that you are a very small cog in a very big wheel. I would like to have from you in concrete form your plans for 1930, not what you think or hope, but what, after careful study and discussion with your board, can really be carried out."

On top of this, she opposed his attendance at the meeting of the American Association of Workers for the Blind at Wawasee, Indiana, and her reasons dealt a blow to his pride. "Where you work your dog for exhibition, your tendency is to show off, and it makes such a bad impression that the effect on a stranger is zero. You make so many inaccurate statements that the public would be in no way benefitted." She suggested that either Dr. Buchanan or Dr. Blair could represent The Seeing Eye far more effectively than Morris.

Jack's report on the Nashville classes was less personal, but equally unflattering. It threw serious doubts on "the business ability of Mr. Frank." It recommended that "much greater care be used in the selection of blind to receive training." Not only should students be physically fit, as Mr. Alexander was not, but the school should be certain "that the man needs the dog as a working helper and not as a plaything."

This latter referred to Dr. Harris and Tartar. When Adelaide Clifford had gone north by way of Savannah to check on him, she reported, "He plays too much with the dog and uses her very little as, having two automobiles and a chauffeur, he has no actual need of a dog other than as a companion."

Jack Humphrey delivered the crowning insult by concluding that whenever a demonstration was necessary, Mr. Rogers and Pal be used in preference to Morris and Buddy. In an accompanying letter to Morris, Dorothy stressed her agreement. "You have let Buddy become so careless and inexact in her work that she is no longer an exhibition dog. I'm sorry, but it is true."

Morris was careful not to rush his answer to Dorothy. He took more than a week to compose a careful reply. He opened humbly: "I deeply appreciate your advice and checkup on my shortcomings. I am sorry that you have taken this attiude toward my attending the convention of the workers for the blind in Wawasee. I feel it is a great mistake not to have The Seeing Eye represented." He understood that Immeln would be the only one with a dog attending, and he would represent, not The Seeing Eye, but the Lighthouse. Carefully he responded to her criticisms one by one, clarifying misuderstandings, but avoiding "dirty digs" or counteroffensives. For once, the letter was faultlessly typed.

Neither Dorothy nor Jack appreciated the magnitude of Morris's problem in trying to recruit classes. Despite inquiries from every state in the union and a massive correspondence, he had found it impossible to find more than one or two candidates in a given city. Even in Nashville, his hometown, where he could deal with applicants face-to-face, he had been able to muster only four students, including the rheumatic and overaged Alexander. He was convinced that it was essential to enlist the cooperation of workers for the blind to recruit classes, and Wawasee was the place to do it. There would not be another convention of the American Assocation of Workers for the Blind until 1931, and he could not afford to wait.

At the last minute, Dorothy Eustis relented and cabled

Morris her approval of his attendance at Wawasee, but it seems certain he was prepared to go with or without her permission. In any case, he was not in Nashville to receive the cable. He was already off on a trip that would take him to Cincinnati, Louisville, and Wawasee.

The first fruits of this important trip were coincidental. Morris was driven by a college classmate, Mike Martin, and they devised a stratagem for getting Buddy into restaurants over the objections of headwaiters. Morris had valid arguments to overcome such objections. Buddy was his eyes. You would not ask a customer to check his eyes outside when he went into the dining room. Buddy was as vital to his mobility as an artificial leg for an amputee. You would not ask a customer to check his wooden leg in the cloakroom. But even the most brilliant reasoning was ineffective with a headwaiter who feared dogs, or feared that the customers feared dogs. So Morris and Mike worked out an alternate plan.

Buddy knew Mike as a good friend. She would naturally seek him out in a crowd of strangers. Therefore, Mike went into the dining room alone and was seated at a table before Morris and Buddy came in. Without consulting the headwaiter, Buddy made for Mike, circling any obstacles, including waiters, as a matter of course. Once Morris was seated with Buddy out of sight beneath the table, the advantage was on his side. It was simpler to serve him than to risk a row before the rest of the customers.

The youth and brashness that were such a handicap in administrative affairs were invaluable in breaking down the barriers against dogs in public places, and breaking down these barriers was essential. Morris was a fighter. He did not mind being conspicuous, and he did not care what means he used to gain his end. Sweet reason and Old World courtesy were useless in this kind of battle. Drs. Buchanan, Blair, and Harris were too conventional for such methods, and even Morris's detractors agree that there was no one in work for the blind who could have done what he did at that time.

Morris freely acknowledges his debt to uninhibited college friends like Mike Martin who were invaluable allies. They regarded the integration of guide dogs in public places as a challenge and a game. Morris recalls entering an all-night diner in Washington with a dozen friends in the small hours. The manager objected to Buddy. One of the boys turned to another. "I don't object to a dog, do you?" The question was relayed around the circle, eliciting one negative after another. When it became clear that the manager was the only one who objected to a dog, they picked him up and carried him outside.

In Cincinnati, Morris's Aunt Selma introduced him to Calvin Glover, president of the American Association of Workers for the Blind. From Glover, Morris learned that Thomas Sinykin, who had imported and retrained Senator Schall's guide dog, was scheduled to speak to the convention and planned to ask for a resolution of support. Morris explained that The Seeing Eye was a nonprofit organization which provided dogs at cost. Sinykin was a businessman seeking a substantial profit. In consequence, the invitation to Sinykin was rescinded and Morris was scheduled in his place. Good luck and Morris's initiative saved the day in the nick of time.

From Cincinnati, Mike drove Morris to Louisville. When Morris and Buddy strode out on the stage before 7,000 Lions, they received a thunderous ovation. Buddy responded with a chorus of barks that put the audience in a good humor. Then Morris gave a short talk modeled on his radio speech, but adding anecdotal material about the classes in Nashville and the successes of the new graduates. He was applauded enthusiastically. The Nashville resolution was proposed and passed. The Seeing Eye had a potential source of recruiters and supporters in every Lions Club from coast to coast.

Morris repeated his success in Wawasee, Indiana. He wrote Mrs. Eustis: "You can talk about your other dogs, madame, but I must salute mine. The corridors are packed with sighted, semisighted, and blind people. She has been stepped upon. She has been kicked, petted, and in many ways annoyed, but at no time did she snap, or bark, or growl. I got through the crowds with less trouble than the sighted people."

In his talk, Morris elaborated on his training in Switzerland, his return trip through New York City, the establishment of The Seeing Eye in Nashville, and the success of the first two classes. He was well received, and when he was finished, a braille teacher from Berkeley, Kate Foley, rose to tell of the feats she had seen performed by Mrs. Eddy and Beda. The most recent issue of *The New Outlook* contained a complimentary article on The Seeing Eye, and the support of Allen and Van Cleve further assisted the movement. Morris reckoned, "The ones who were on the fence are now in favor of it, and the 40% who did not favor it are now either in favor or on the fence. I do not believe that anyone at the convention is actually opposed to it." Van Cleve had written Jessie Frank, "We are all very proud of Morris and the splendid manner in which he put over his proposition."

Morris's informal contacts at the convention were as important as his public presentation. He met Mary Dranga Campbell, the ex-wife of Charles Campbell and executive secretary of the Missouri State Commission for the Blind. She had earlier written to Morris in Nashville about an applicant for a dog. Only now did Morris realize that the applicant was Mervyn Sinclair, the president of the Pennsylvania Council for the Blind, where Mary Campbell had previously worked. Sinclair would be as valuable a convert as Herbert Immeln, and Morris reported, "I have offered him an opening in the class we are planning to hold in the last part of November in Birmingham, Alabama."

He had been delighted to meet Herbert Immeln, too.

Immeln said the Lighthouse was thinking of building kennels, which would make it an ideal place for Adelaide Clifford to train six dogs for the Birmingham class. The July class under Weber, sponsored by the Lighthouse, was about to begin, and it seemed to offer a pattern of cooperation for the future. As managing director in the Nashville headquarters, Morris would correspond with the appropriate local agency, which would line up a class of students in its city. From Lake Openaka, Willi Ebeling would locate suitable dogs for Adelaide or Herr Weber to train, and they would then take the dogs to the city in question to hold the class.

Morris could feel well satisfied that his trip to Wawasee had won important gains. The savor of success was the sweeter for having been won over the objections of Dorothy Eustis. He returned to Nashville riding high and confident of the future, but the Lighthouse "plan" failed to take certain factors into account. There was no clearly defined division of authority and responsibility between the Lighthouse and The Seeing Eye. Willi Ebeling's role was not understood by Immeln, Weber, or even Morris, and Weber was still an unknown quantity. Under the circumstances, there was every likelihood of serious trouble.

Even before the class began, relations between Willi Ebeling and Morris Frank were strained. Willi was finding his work load much heavier than he had anticipated. "I seem to have time for nothing but Seeing Eye business." In addition to advising Morris, he was responsible for analyzing and solving by letter the problems of graduates in the field. Although she had been shown in Nashville, Mrs. Eddy did not know how to board a streetcar. Earl Pendleton's Muddles was becoming crowd-shy in the noise and confusion of the Tennessee School for the Blind. Letters to correct such problems had to be explicit, tactful, and carefully composed.

Ebeling's search for suitable dogs involved long auto-

mobile trips for which his expenses were inadequately re-
imbursed. He did not lack for money, but he was a stickler
for precision, and Morris's lapses irritated him. "I want to
help, Morris, but I am not going to do your work for you."
From Immeln he learned that Morris had quoted him in-
discreetly at Wawasee. "Put a padlock on your mouth, and
talk with your brain!"

Adelaide Clifford was also dissatisfied with Morris. She
had enjoyed her New York class, but the uncertainties of
the future were galling. At different times, Morris had asked
her tentatively to take classes in Trenton, Pittsburgh, Cincinnati, Birmingham, Berkeley, and San Francisco, but nothing was definite.

Although Willi Ebeling had suggested Weber in the
first instance, the two Germans were not sympathetic. Willi
drove over to Princeton with Adelaide to watch Weber take
his blindfold tests. By the time Weber got to his third dog,
Willi wrote Morris, he "was staggering like a drunken man.
We had a good laugh at his expense." On his side, Weber
resented supervision. He had been training dogs twice as
long as Willi Ebeling and Adelaide Clifford combined.

The truth was that Weber's years of experience were
a handicap rather than an asset. They had been devoted to
a kind of training that inculcated prompt and precise obedience. Such obedience was unsuitable for a guide, which
must have the freedom to disobey commands that might be
dangerous. Even if its blind master commanded it, a guide
must not lead him forward into an open manhole, an overhanging awning, or a stream of speeding cars. Teaching a
dog to make decisions required a completely different approach than training it to obey.

This difference of approach explained the necessity for
the blindfold test. With their extraordinary sensory acuity,
dogs learning to guide are keenly aware of the body language
of their instructors. Approaching an obstacle, a sighted instructor might slacken his pace almost imperceptibly or
shift his balance ever so slightly, preparing to turn right or

left. The instructor might be entirely unaware of such a body signal, but to an alert dog it would constitute a command as clear as the spoken word. Having obeyed this silent and unconscious command, the dog would be rewarded by its instructor's praise, "Atta good girl!" and reinforced to do the same again when opportunity presented. Under a blindfold, an instructor could not anticipate visible obstacles and a dog would have to solve its guiding problems on its own initiative without benefit of body signals.

The Seeing Eye's educational philosophy applied even to the teaching of obedience exercises. Instant obedience was not required because for a guide dog, every command contains an element of request. The dog must be allowed a moment to think it over. "Forward" means "Forward if you think it's a good idea." If you teach that "Down" means "Down!" Right away! No matter what!" you may form the habit that "Forward" means "Forward! No matter what!" even when a car is coming.

Educating through a sensitive grasp of dog psychology is far more demanding than training by means of corporal punishment. In Nashville, Jack Humphrey had tried to explain Seeing Eye methods to Weber in teaching obedience to Anitra and Betty, but, Jack recalled, "One day when I wasn't looking, he put on the spikes and spoiled everything." The "spikes" referred to a training collar with spikes on the inside used to enforce obedience. At the time they were common enough in other types of training, but anathema to The Seeing Eye. This incident probably explains why Jack was insistent that Weber's dogs be checked by Willi Ebeling and Adelaide Clifford.

Immeln had lined up three men for Weber's class: a student at Harvard Law named Prendergast; Carl Wartenburg of Brooklyn, who caned chairs; and Peter Gillen of Astoria, who was unemployed. They had heard from Morris by letter, but their direct contact was confined to Lighthouse personnel and, during the first days of the class, to

Weber. The Seeing Eye was for them only a shadowy entity in the background.

Weber opened the class on July 4. At that time the sale of fireworks was unrestricted, and Willi Ebeling disapproved. "It is too risky to have strange dogs and strange people in a strange location on such a noisy day. One firecracker tied to a dog's tail, and he would never come home."

On July 9, he drove three hours through the summer heat to inspect the class on the streets of Astoria. He found Prendergast paired with Gretel, Wartenburg with Blackie, and Gillen with Asta. His reaction toward Weber was immediate, unequivocal, and negative. He announced, "I have come to the conclusion we do not want him. I am not going to comment on his work, but he has an insubordinate character which does not fit into our plans. I had a disagreement with him. He had changed his schedule, and I had to make him work one dog a second time that afternoon. He was abusive, and I will have nothing further to do with him."

Since the first student had worked before he arrived, Willi was fully justified in asking him to work again. It was a matter of only a few minutes, and when Weber protested, he asserted his authority. Two Teutonic temperaments sizzled in the heat. But it was more than a matter of temperament. It was a question of safety. He had seen evidence of unsound technique, but he did not attempt to describe it to Morris, who would be unable to grasp the subtleties. Unfortunately, his way of putting it to Morris was simply "I am not going to comment on his work," which left Morris with the impression that it was only Weber's "insubordinate character" to which Willi objected. Weber's students were similarly in the dark about the role of this stranger who had quarreled with their instructor.

Adelaide was due to come down from Maine for an inspection, and Willi's instinct was to remove Weber and turn the class over to her. It would cost something, but

"The success of the class is more important than a few dollars." Moreover, having found Weber unsatisfactory, he did not want him to finish a class, because that might seem to confer The Seeing Eye's stamp of approval. He was absolutely convinced that "Weber some day will be a competitor."

His conviction was doubtless correct. It was certainly to Weber's advantage to sever connections with The Seeing Eye. It was an infant organization struggling along on a shoestring. The Lighthouse was a flourishing and well-endowed institution with an operating budget of a half-million dollars a year. Weber knew that Immeln was already raising money for a second class and would need an instructor. If he remained with The Seeing Eye, Weber's work would be under the constant supervision of Willi Ebeling or Adelaide Clifford. With the Lighthouse, he could train as he pleased with no nonsense about blindfold tests.

Willi Ebeling postponed any decision until Adelaide had made her inspection. Probably at Weber's suggestion, Immeln was present for that inspection. Like Morris, Immeln worked well with his own dog, and it would have been easy for him to believe that this gave him a knowledge of guide-dog instruction.

As Immeln described it to Morris, Prendergast worked Gretel on the sidewalk while Willi and Adelaide watched, "driving along in Mr. Ebeling's machine. The dog reached the corner and slanted to the other side." (That is, Gretel crossed the intersection diagonally.) "Miss Clifford jumped from the machine and told Mr. Weber to make the dog do it over again. Mr. Weber said, no, they would do it at the next corner."

Adelaide called Willi Ebeling from his car, and a heated argument ensued in front of Prendergast. Immeln reported, "Mr. Ebeling and Miss Clifford were handling Mr. Weber as if they were dealing with a low type of servant

instead of a human being." Presumably, he did not appreciate how very wrong Weber was. Diagonal crossing of an
intersection is extremely dangerous in traffic. Even on a
deserted street, it will confuse the master's orientation and
tend to make him lose his way

Even more important, the time to correct an error is at
the moment it occurs. This is a fundamental and inflexible
rule of guide-dog education. A single wrong impression can
ruin a dog. Weber's refusal to make the correction then
and there was inexcusable. The only plausible explanation
is that he was trying to provoke an open break between
The Seeing Eye and the Lighthouse.

Willi Ebeling had full authority to discharge Weber
and put the class under Adelaide, but there were two obstacles in the way. The first was the confidence of the students. "Weber has poisoned the minds of the blind against
us and tells them that we know nothing and that he knows
it all." The second was the division of authority between
the Lighthouse and The Seeing Eye. Immeln repeatedly
insisted that the class was under Lighthouse "supervision,"
a word to which Morris had consented. As Willi wrote
him, "When you use such a word, you must define what
you mean. If you had used the word 'auspices,' you would
have taken some of the authority away."

Caught in an untenable position, Willi Ebeling com-
promised. After a three-hour conference with Immeln, he
agreed to let Weber complete the class without supervision
by Adelaide. In return, she was to have absolute authority
to pass or fail each man-dog unit at the end of the class.
This reserved to The Seeing Eye the all-important right to
insist on safety.

Willi reported all this to Morris in a long letter and
repeated earlier requests that Morris forward to him copies
of any letters he had received from either Immeln or Weber.
Morris had a letter from Immeln, but instead of sending
a copy to Willi Ebeling, he discussed it with two members

of his board. He "didn't deem it wise" to send on Immeln's letter. He therefore withheld it and telephoned Immeln in New York to mediate long-distance.

Morris was meddling where he had no business. This was a question of training, and in Jack Humphrey's absence, Willi Ebeling was responsible for all training matters. Morris had returned to his old habit of asking advice from people unqualified to give it. His board members, who knew nothing about training, advised him to telephone Immeln, who also knew nothing about training. Worse yet, he accepted Immeln's version of events rather than Willi Ebeling's. He wrote Dorothy, "I feel that Herr Weber has received the most unfair treatment and that if he had received the proper cooperation, he could have finished the class." After talking to Immeln, Morris sent a wire, not to Willi Ebeling, but to Adelaide Clifford.

"No mail since your arrival in New York. Send a report at once on working of dogs and blind masters. Also suggestions on anything that is necessary. Take no action without first asking my approval. Situation delicate."

Willie Ebeling was incensed. The mention of no mail ignored his very detailed reports or implied they were useless. Of the statement, "Take no action without first asking my approval," he wired Morris, "My interpretation is that you disapprove of my action. As I have fulfilled my promise, my supervision is ended with the day."

Morris was stricken at Willi Ebeling's resignation and tried to smooth matters over on the telephone, but he still seemed inclined to side with Immeln. He wrote Dorothy, "Mr. Immeln said he felt very friendly toward me," but "speaking for himself as well as his organization, as long as Mr. Ebeling is in any way connected, the Lighthouse will have nothing else to do with The Seeing Eye. Mr. Immeln also said that Herr Weber would train the next class." Perhaps Morris still felt some faint hope of a reconciliation.

In fairness to Morris, it must be admitted that the

prospect of cooperation was very tempting. Fresh from his triumphs with the International Lions and the A.A.W.B., he was emboldened to try his hand at diplomacy with Ebeling and Immeln. From his perspective it looked more like a clash of temperaments than of principles.

From Mt. Pelerin, Dorothy saw more clearly. She wholly backed Willi Ebeling and Adelaide, who had properly focused on The Seeing Eye's single overriding objective: "the safety of the blind man. This point must be kept in mind first, last, and all the time." She concluded that neither Weber nor Immeln grasped the basic principles of guide-dog education and should have no place in the school's future plans. If there were to be any cooperation with other agencies in the future, The Seeing Eye's absolute responsibility for training would have to be spelled out clearly.

Willi Ebeling relented somewhat from his original telegram of resignation and shared with Adelaide in judging the safety of the three students. They passed on all three, though somewhat reluctantly on Gillen with Asta. Willi further agreed to make Openaka available to Adelaide and her next string of dogs during training, and even to put up a Swiss trainer from L'Oeil Qui Voit, but he made his position with Morris clear in a letter of August 4. "Now, Morris, life is too short for me to waste my time the way I have been wasting it with fruitless attempts at helping you. In another capacity, I shall still continue to be some help to The Seeing Eye for a bit, but no more of this. You will have to find a better man than I am and one you can trust more."

Dorothy Eustis wrote Morris a string of deliberately embarrassing questions. "If you have cut yourself off from further assistance from Mr. Ebeling, will you let me know how you plan to collect your dogs, attend to the shipping, kennels, etc.? how you plan to inspect the work, advise the men, etc., if you have not Mr. Ebeling as supervisor? I am afraid you have left yourself in a very unfortunate position." It was her way of driving home to Morris how very much the school depended on Willi Ebeling's invaluable assistance.

Willi had been deeply hurt by Morris's loss of trust in him, his readiness to consult members of his board, Herbert Immeln, and Adelaide Clifford rather than himself. But the six months he had devoted to The Seeing Eye had made a true believer of him. The Seeing Eye and Morris needed him. He could not resist that need. On August 9, only five days after having told Morris to find someone else, he wrote again to say, "The Lighthouse is a dead issue with me." The letter went on with pages of the most detailed advice as to how to arrange for classes in Berkeley and San Francisco in 1930. Willi Ebeling was hooked, and he knew it. The Seeing Eye would consume all his considerable talents and energies for the next twenty-five years.

CHAPTER 7

L'Oeil
Qui Voit

"QUITE NATURALLY people are asking me about The Seeing Eye, and I have been doing my level best to put them straight. The point is, however, I am stumped with the many questions I am asked."

Writing in September 1929, Adelaide Clifford poured out to Dorothy Eustis her perplexity about the confused affairs of The Seeing Eye. People are surprised, she wrote, because there seems to be "no real head to make the movement go except a charming woman who is on a Swiss mountain top thousands of miles away. Funny that a new organization should be put in the hands of a young boy twenty-one years old, and the organization has but one trainer to start the work here with, and that trainer at that a young girl. Why hasn't there been more progress in the movement? Why doesn't The Seeing Eye find trainers in this country?" A series of questions followed culminating in the "one big question, why you, the president of the organization, don't come over here and see to it that things are run the way they ought to be?"

Dorothy Eustis answered immediately with her usual candor. The Seeing Eye "was put in the hands of a blind boy of twenty-one, because he was the only one who had the guts to touch it." The Red Cross, the American Foundation for the Blind, the Lighthouse, and the Philadelphia School for the Blind had all turned down her offers to bring guide dogs to America.

The reason there had not been more progress was the difficulty of finding trainers. If she trained Americans they would demand wages that would put the price of a guide dog out of reach. She was well aware that things were not being run properly, but there was no point in her coming to the United States and arousing interest until she had the trainers to make good on her promises. This work was for the benefit of the blind "and not to provide dinner conversation for the seeing."

Meanwhile, "The Swiss mountain top on which I am supposed to be sitting is the last place where anyone could find time to sit, and we are learning far more by having the Lausanne school developing under our noses than in a hundred trips to Germany."

At this writing, the school in Lausanne had been going for four months. At the invitation of Mussolini, Dorothy had spent March and April in Rome overseeing a course for Italian police. Jack Humphrey had not returned from Nashville until May. In the interim, Captain Balsiger had prepared his house and kennels to quarter blind students, apprentices, and dogs. With the mediation of her secretary Gretchen Green, Dorothy had negotiated with Italian and French authorities to supply both military and civilian blind to be trained. L'Oeil Qui Voit officially opened it doors on June 2.

In July, Dorothy and Jack attended the International Conference for the Blind in Vienna, and Dorothy was named chairman of a commission to study the use and practicability of the dog as leader for the blind. The commission would report to the next international conference in 1931. Another delegate in Vienna was Robert Irwin of the American Foundation. During a visit to Fortunate Fields, Dorothy wrote, "Mr. Irwin went over every day to Lausanne to take a walk with one of the dogs in training. He is personally very much in favor of the work, but I do not think he is ready yet to give the endorsement of the American Foundation."

Balsiger was only the administrative head of L'Oeil Qui Voit. Humphrey was its guiding genius. His restless mind was soon making improvements on German methods. German dogs were taught to bark at pedestrians who blocked their path. This would have frightened Americans, and Jack's dogs were taught to work silently. In some phases of the training, Germans used slaps as a means of correcting their dogs. Jack found this sort of corporal punishment to be unnecessary and undesirable, for it might inculcate unthinking obedience. In the course of time, Jack devised literally scores of further modifications.

Some interesting cultural problems arose in the training of French and Italian blind veterans. In a mixed class, they spent so much time arguing about who had won the war that they had to be trained separately thereafter. Basic to training in any language was the necessity of rewarding a dog verbally for every desirable act and doing it with sufficient expression to carry meaning to the dog. French and Swiss students seemed to have no difficulty, but the Italians were listless with their praise. When reminded, they would shrug, "But a dog has no soul."

The Marchesa Cavalletti, a friend of Dorothy's, hit on the solution. Italians should be asked to view their dogs in the context, not of theology, but of theater. All Italians understood the audience's obligation to applaud a good performance, and their rewards for their guides soon rang with the gusto of curtain calls at La Scala.

The French objected to using German shepherds and insisted on sending the school a variety of French dogs, all of which proved unsuitable. "The poodles were the most interesting, as they were amazingly quick to learn, but oh so la-de-da! They were totally lacking in a feeling of responsibility for the person they were leading. If something caught their attention, they would go right over a curb or drop their trainer into a hole."

These are the comments of still another remarkable personality whom Dorothy Eustis attracted to Fortunate Fields. She was Edith "Missy" Doudge, a strikingly attractive young horsewoman from Virginia, who spoke both Italian and French fluently. Dorothy felt she would be a natural with animals and, against Jack's will, persuaded him to give her a try. Jack considered her "a slip of a young lady" without the stamina for the work, and he decided to give her rough treatment. "When I thought I had her discouraged with a trip under blindfold behind a strange and hard-pulling dog in the heaviest of Lausanne traffic for better than an hour I told her to pull the blindfold and asked her, 'Well, what do you think?' She looked clear through me with cold blue eyes and said, 'I think I like it.' To make a long story short, in a few months, she was in charge of the training and cut a big work load from my shoulders."

Jack expressed the philosophy of L'Oeil Qui Voit in a letter to Adelaide Clifford. "You can learn something from each dog and each blind man you come in contact with. Keep your eyes and ears and mind open, and learn, learn, learn. Your work will constantly get better, and you will constantly find the work more interesting. That is why I like the breeding and training of animals. Every mating, every animal is a new problem and offers something new to be learned."

What Jack was learning might have been lost, but for an idea triggered by Gretchen Green. One day, Dorothy told Jack she wanted him to go to Paris to see a woman named Helen Hubbard. "Just that," he recalled, "and not what to see her about." Needless to say, Helen Hubbard was another of Gretchen's wealthy friends.

He went, saw Helen Hubbard, and answered questions. Then she announced that there was something she wished to finance. To guarantee that the knowledge Jack was accumulating should be preserved in permanent form, she (with an assist from Dorothy) would subsidize Jack in the writing of two scientific reports "as time allowed."

Both reports were written. The first, in collaboration with Lucien Warner, was published as *Working Dogs* in 1934. The second was completed in 1938. It was in the form of a series of lectures on 3,000 typewritten pages, illustrated with hundreds of photographs, and collected in twenty notebooks. They constitute the gospel according to Jack Humphrey on the education of dogs, students, and instructors at The Seeing Eye.

Jack carefully defined the qualities desired in a guide dog. In addition to good health and the appropriate size, strength, and stamina, a guide must have willingness and intelligence. Appearance can be deceiving. One dog seemed lacking in intelligence because she was playing dumb. With another instructor who put up with no nonsense, she proved highly intelligent. Jack warned that if an apprentice found his dog's intelligence rating going down during training, it was a sign his dog was thinking faster than he was.

When a stubborn dog was put under an instructor who disliked her, she soon refused to work at all. Under an instructor free from personal dislike, her willingness increased markedly. It became a rule that no instructor should work with a dog he disliked. Jack believed that "the dog or horse or any other animal which is stubborn makes much the better worker, once the stubbornness is overcome, than the animal who never gave any trouble. I am always afraid of the future with any animal which does not set its will again mine for a while."

Shyness was the most undesirable trait. A guide must be absolutely "gun-sure"—not startled by sudden or loud noises or overly sensitive to body pain. On the other hand, a dog with too low sensitivity of either ear or body was difficult to reach. For best results, a dog should be medium sensitive to sound and touch.

Too keen a sense of smell was a handicap. One dog so willing that she was able to take fifteen blind men for a walk in a single afternoon was so sensitive to the scent of pigeons that she would give chase even to one she could not see around a corner.

A guide dog requires sufficient aggressiveness to lead its master through crowds and to stand its ground steadily between two lines of moving traffic. Yet it must be willing to tolerate jostling and the unwelcome attentions and caresses of what Jack called "old ladies of both sexes."

Working Dogs reported the case of Fortunate Fields Dog 315. When its character was tested at twelve, fifteen, and eighteen months, it was found to lack sufficient aggressiveness for police work. As a guide, the dog worked well until the apprentice put on a blindfold. It then headed for the shade of a tree and lay down. If the man under blindfold was being watched by a sighted instructor, Dog 315 worked. When not under observation, it was back to the shade of the tree. Having failed as a guide, it was sent back to Fortunate Fields for another chance at police work. By sheer accident, a trainer lying in ambush for a different dog mistakenly staged a mock attack on Dog 315 and its trainer. To the surprise of all concerned, it sprang ferociously to the defense. The dog's entire character had changed in the interval between eighteen and thirty-three months. It was later trained as a hard attack dog.

Jack found that a dog's ability to learn was almost unlimited if the dog could be made to understand what its master wanted. For guide work, this required the instructor to "get inside the dog's mind." In other types of training, the man imposed his will on the dog from above. In the education of a guide dog, the instructor must understand the dog's point of view and work, not down from the man, but up from the dog.

After learning to pull in harness, a dog is taught to stop at curbs. A curb is no obstacle for a dog, and it is natural for her to run right over it. To show her this is wrong, the instructor pretends to stumble, tramples his feet noisily, and utters the worst imprecation in a guide dog's vocabulary, *"Pfui!"* It is spoken with venom, and the dog is immediately aware that something is terribly wrong. The instructor steps backward on to the curb, calls the dog to come and sit on his left side. Her obedient response is rewarded with an "Atta good girl" as joyous as the *"Pfui"* was angry. The dog is pleased.

The instructor then commands her "Forward." The moment she moves, she receives another "Atta good girl!," but just when she thinks everything is going swimmingly, she runs the curb on the opposite side of the street. Again trampling feet and a terrible *"Pfui!"* Again, "Come" and "Sit" are rewarded with ecstatic "Atta good girls!" In only a few repetitions, the dog is aware that there is something potentially very dangerous about a curb. She slows and stops warily several feet away. The instructor commands, *"Hopp, hopp!"* This German phrase is roughly translatable as "Go on," or "Keep going." It is spoken in an encouraging tone and with a forward gesturing of the right hand. If the dog does not understand, the instructor may swing his right leg around and nudge her in the hindquarters with his toe. This is not a kick or a punishment, only a gentle physical reinforcement of a command she does not understand. The moment she moves forward, there is another "Atta good girl!" and when she comes to a stop at the curb this is repeated joyously and accompanied by a few pats.

Timing, consistency, and total concentration on the dog are everything. When they fail, a dog gets the wrong idea of what is wanted. One apprentice seemed to be working well with a dog. Jack noted that when she sat for curbs and obstacles, he rewarded her with *"Oui, il est beau!"*— the French equivalent of "Atta good girl!" Jack took her for a test walk and found when he rewarded her for swerving to avoid an oncoming pedestrian, the dog sat down. It developed that the apprentice had forgotten to reward her for any act except sitting at curbs and barriers. As a result, she came to think that *"Oui, il est beau!"* meant "Sit!" The mistake was inconsistency, the failure to reward *every* desired act rather than those of a particular category.

Concentration on the dog's reactions is as important as consistency. Well-meaning dog lovers with kind hearts but no understanding of guide-dog technique can be troublesome for instructors. They may interpret the nudge with the toe as a kick and try to interfere. One apprentice working his dog up to a curb noticed two elderly ladies who looked like interfering types. When his dog ran the curb, he trampled his feet in the prescribed manner, but stepped on her paw in the process. She gave a yelp of pain, and to forestall the protests of the ladies, he lavished her with the most extravagant and undeserved praises and pats. He was thinking of their effect on the human observers, but they made an even deeper impression on the dog.

When they reached the next down curb, she repeated the yelp of pain that had evoked such unstinting rewards at the previous corner. The association was so firmly embedded in her mind that she could never be broken of yelping at every down curb and had to be retired from training.

Many of the anecdotes cited in this chapter may seem negative. They describe mistakes, but they illustrate the extraordinary sensitivity of dogs in training, and their net impact was wholly positive, because the school learned from every mistake. Nor have I confined my examples to the experience of L'Oeil Qui Voit in 1929. The learning experience was the same on both sides of the Atlantic, and has never ceased.

Jack Humphrey insisted that teaching conditions approximate the realities the blind student would encounter beyond the school. He taught a Swiss girl to work without using a cane because at home she would need her right hand for carrying a briefcase. In training, however, she nearly defeated the purpose. Instead of using the prescribed method for making her dog sit for curbs, she was using her right hand to give the leash an upward jerk. This was easy at L'Oeil Qui Voit, but would be very awkward later when she was encumbered with a briefcase.

One American apprentice ignored reality in another way. To correct a dog who failed to give sufficient clearance for parking meters on his right, he used the prescribed formula, slapping the meter with a *"Pfui"* and, as soon as his dog moved left, rewarding her with an "Atta good girl." This correction was within the power of a blind master, but the apprentice went on to give positive reinforcement in a way a blind master could not. He rewarded his dog every time she cleared a meter successfully, although a blind person could not have known that the meter was there. During a blindfold test, the error was revealed. When the dog had cleared three meters without receiving her customary reward, she decided her man did not know where the meters were. To show him, she bumped him into every other meter on the block.

Even under blindfold, it was possible for an instructor to give body cues that would cause problems for a later master. One apprentice unconsciously encouraged a somewhat unwilling dog with a slight lift on the harness handle on the command of "Forward." The dog learned to respond, not to the verbal command, but to the lift. When she was paired with a blind master, she would not budge on command.

Sometimes trouble resulted from circumstances beyond control. Fortunate Fields Dog 270 tested as gun-sure and was paired successfully to a war veteran. Some months later as they were waiting at a curb, a truck backfired almost in the dog's face. The veteran, a victim of shellshock, screamed, started backward, stepped on his dog's paw, and fell on her. The ear pain reinforced by her body pain and the contagion of her master's fright proved traumatic. Dog 270 became too sound-sensitive for safety and had to be replaced.

With his keen eye and active mind, Jack was continually discovering new subtleties and refinements of guide-dog technique. He had something new to tell his lady boss almost every day. Therefore, although Dorothy was sometimes unhappy about the slowness of progress in America, she was confident that the work of L'Oeil Qui Voit was laying a foundation of knowledge on which the American school would build. In addition to this grounding in theory and practice, L'Oeil Qui Voit was about to graduate its first apprentice instructor for The Seeing Eye.

On the
Road

GEORGES GUILLAUME LOUIS DEBETAZ was born in Lausanne on May 20, 1906. In the spring of 1929, with the Collège Scientifique and his military service behind him, he was looking for work when an old friend of the family, Major Champod, told him about L'Oeil Qui Voit. Champod was a police officer who had worked with Mrs. Eustis and would be happy to recommend young Debetaz as an apprentice.

Debetaz knew nothing about dogs and less about blind people, but one point in Champod's story made him prick up his cars. An apprentice instructor from L'Oeil Qui Voit was likely to be sent to the United States.

It was a period when many young Swiss emigrated to foreign countries in search of economic opportunity, and those who returned on vacation cut a wide swath. Debetaz recalls them "flashing their money all over Creation." It was not a love of dogs nor an altruistic concern for blind people, but the lure of the Yankee dollar that prompted him to enroll in the school. He launched on a lifelong career without the faintest idea of what it entailed.

Jack Humphrey was not impressed by the blond Swiss in the jaunty beret. His wiry physique seemed too frail and his temperament too anxious. "When they order me into the box with the dog," Debetaz recalls, "I was not anxious. I was scared stiff."

Jack had predicted he would not last a week, but of the scores of young men who enrolled in L'Oeil Qui Voit, Debetaz was the first of only three to graduate to the rank of instructor. He lasted not a week, but forty-three years, and with one exception, he possessed in abundance all the qualities of the ideal instructor.

Some of these qualities, notably intelligence, willingness, and physical stamina, were also qualities of the ideal guide dog. Physically, an instructor must be strong enough to control a dog, but size was no advantage. Indeed, if it interfered with quickness and agility, it was a handicap. In practice, the ideal height for an instructor proved to be from five feet, six inches to five feet, ten, on a frame that carried no excess fat.

An instructor could not be afraid of hard work. The work day ranged from ten to twelve hours a day, six days a week. An instructor walked about ten miles a day at three and a half miles an hour, training as many as ten dogs in a string. These dogs must also be given obedience exercises, curried, fed, and watered. During classes, instructors were on call twenty-four hours a day for three or four weeks.

The training of guide dogs required mental concentration of a high order, the imagination to see things from a dog's point of view, and the ability to communicate with a dog. Those who had these qualities often failed for lack of the ability to communicate with blind humans. During class, the blind students were frequently under a severe strain. Their anxiety made it hard for them to understand. Directions to such students must be clear and precise. A degree of sympathy was important, but somewhat surprisingly, too much patience was a failing. If they were allowed to make the same mistakes over and over again by a forbearing teacher, neither dogs nor humans learned as well as from one who insisted on real effort.

Good nerves were another prerequisite. Instructors

generally worked two students at a time. Keeping an eye on
two uncertain students working strange dogs around routes
that combined pedestrian and automobile traffic with steps,
barriers, obstructions, and overhangs could be harrowing,
and many trainers dropped out from sheer nervous exhaus-
tion. From the experience of the German schools, Dorothy
and Jack concluded that only 5 to 8 percent of all apprentices ever completed training.

Young Debetaz progressed admirably, and as early as
August, Mrs. Eustis was writing Morris of a Swiss she was
prepared to send over to work under Adelaide. Morris de-
murred. Bank failures in Birmingham had wiped out the
savings of both the prospective students and the sponsoring
agency for the class, and he doubted he had enough work
for a second instructor. Later, however, when Mervyn Sinclair and the Pennsylvania Council for the Blind were able
to assemble a class in Harrisburg for November, Debetaz was
sent for posthaste. He had just time for a ten-day course in
English at the Berlitz School before he sailed.

Jack wrote Adelaide, "You will not have trouble with
him taking orders from anybody else, since he will not learn
English until he gets over there, and you will be the only
one who can really talk to him." In his native Lausanne,
Debetaz had all the qualities of the ideal instructor. In his
new country, he would have a problem communicating with
his English-speaking students.

On November 8, he saw the Statue of Liberty, raising
her lamp "beside the Golden Door" just as the United
States was to enter the worst depression in its history. Willi
Ebeling met the boat and drove the young Swiss back to
Openaka, where he was installed in "the help house" and
given board, lodging, and seventy-five dollars a month. In
return he worked a seventy- to eighty-hour week. Each
morning and afternoon, Adelaide drove him into Morristown in her cream-color convertible Auburn with wire
wheels, and they trained eight dogs on the streets. What
with their other responsibilities in caring for the dogs,

Adelaide wrote Morris, "I don't have time to write letters even to my own mother."

Adelaide had taken time earlier in the fall to make her debut in New York, but now her work was cut out for her. A week after Debetaz's arrival, she sprained her foot giving a curb correction. Willi Ebeling wrote Morris to postpone the class for two weeks, but even with this additional time, preparations encountered difficulty.

Two of the dogs in Adelaide's string had been graduated before: Betty with Hedrick and Asta with Gillen. Hedrick had returned Betty because his landlord objected to her. For submitting without a fight, Morris had declared Hedrick "yellow to the core" and barred him from admission to any class in the future. Gillen had spoiled Asta by playing with her at home and failing to reward her work on the streets. According to her logic, Gillen loved her only at home, so Asta sought to keep him there and refused to work. Betty accepted retraining, but toward the end of November, Adelaide decided that her attempt to rehabilitate Asta had failed.

"I got her to work well, but she is unsafe and won't work for anyone but me, so I don't want to take chances."

Willi wired Morris that he would have to cut one of the students from the Harrisburg class. Morris groaned. Having sold the virtues of the guide dog to the members of the class, he now had to dash the hopes of one of them. Willi suggested offering him a place in Morristown in February or March with one of the two new dogs Debetaz was training.

As a candidate for Debetaz's second dog, Willi wrote Morris, "There is a local blind man, a Negro, and someone wants to collect for getting him a dog. If he is a deserving Negro, what is to be done about it?"

The young man whose family had had George Washington Carver to dinner knew exactly where he stood on race. He answered, "Have him write to the office and put him through the same routine as the rest. We are an organization to furnish dogs for the deserving blind, and I do not think we can discriminate and still call ourselves a non-profit organization." Willi responded, "I just wanted to know whether the organization had drawn a color line. I did not think so, but I wanted to be sure."

In this brief exchange, The Seeing Eye policy on race was settled once for all in 1929. As late as the 1950s, an association for the blind in a southern city used to post sighted monitors at the entrance for its Christmas party, so that the blind guests who could not see each other's color would be able to segregate racially.

Of the five remaining students in the class, Morris was particularly anxious for success with three workers for the blind. In addition to Mervyn Sinclair of the Pennsylvania Council, they were Ann Connelly of Burlington, Vermont, and Sadie Jacobs of New Orleans. He warned Adelaide that Miss Jacobs was "a very small nervous person" and she was bringing her secretary with her, which might pose a problem. Adelaide was optimistic. "Yesterday I put Debetaz through his first blindfold test with me. The dogs worked tic-tac, so three cheers!" She and Debetaz twice had dinner in restaurants in order to teach their dogs to lie quietly under the table. "Debetaz is doing very well. He will have two dogs to work every day in Harrisburg, and, believe me, I am going to keep him busy. He is an awfully nice fellow and very willing."

On December 14, Adelaide and Debetaz drove to Harrisburg over ice-covered roads. There had been difficulty finding a place for Adelaide to stay where she could be properly chaperoned. The Y.W.C.A. was "too awful a place," and through Mr. Sinclair she found a room in the River View Manor. The following morning they picked up the crates with seven dogs at the railroad station. The class assembled at the Hotel Colonial in the afternoon. Besides the three workers for the blind, it included the Reverend C. E. Seymour from Baltimore and Clyde Hutley, a piano tuner from Jamestown, New York. Adelaide read a letter of greeting from Morris and had the students sign a contract agreeing not to sell or breed their dogs. Mr. Hutley did not know how to write and signed his with an X. The distribution of the dogs went well except for Miss Jacobs. "She is afraid of dogs which makes it very difficult." Harrisburg was much larger than Adelaide had imagined and would present some problems.

A few days later, she reported that the class had agreed to work on Saturday and Sunday, so as to have two days off for Christmas. "Miss Jacobs appears to have forgotten to be afraid of her dog, and the situation looks brighter, but she is so small compared to the dog. She doesn't seem strong enough to hold her. She is a little bit of a woman and only weighs ninety-six pounds. The dog is almost as big as she is. She has to run to keep up." Sinclair was doing remarkably well. "Every one is very much in love with their dogs, and all the dogs are working well. Debetaz is having an English lesson with Rev. Seymour every night for a half hour. I am so busy with the blind that I find very little time to talk to him at all."

At the end of the first week, Fox Movietone News took films of Mervyn Sinclair with Kara. Adelaide tried to postpone the filming until the class was more advanced. Things were going quite well, but Adelaide was beginning to wonder whether it would not be a good idea to have Willi Ebeling come to Harrisburg to check the class.

Morris reported to Adelaide that he had most enthusiastic letters about the course from Ann Connelly and Mervyn Sinclair and hoped the others were doing as well. In Vevey the year before, Morris had bought a braille watch, something not available in the States. He had ordered a shipment of them from the same jeweler and would be happy to make them available at cost to any of the students who wanted them.

A couple of days later, Adelaide wrote that "Sinclair is working beautifully with his dog, and I am more than pleased with him. He is really one of the nicest men I have ever worked with. His dog Kara has won him absolutely. Everybody else is doing very well except Miss Jacobs. Morris, she just simply can't seem to hold her dog as she is not strong enough. How to put enough strength in that left arm of hers is out of my line. I am doing my darndest to find a way out for her. She is certainly one terrible case.

Morris reported on a letter from Sadie Jacobs: she was "in love with her dog" and making a strenuous effort to make good in her work, not only for herself, but for the host of friends who are all awaiting her return, and she couldn't possibly disappoint them. But Adelaide answered that "we have had a terrible time with her and still are. Up until today, she has worked like the devil. The big trouble now is that her dog is just about ruined and refuses to work for her. I am doing everything possible, but nothing seems to work."

In desperation, Adelaide finally appealed to Willi Ebeling. He came to Harrisburg and observed for two days, then ruled that it was hopeless. "The case is such a pathetic one. A long trip for nothing. However, the fault lies absolutely with Miss Jacobs."

He composed a detailed analysis of the case. Her dog, a good worker with very strong nerves, "stood the gaff as long as it could, then gave up and absolutely refused to do anything. Adelaide and Debetaz tried everything, and nothing would go. When I got to Harrisburg, both were nervous wrecks over the case."

Miss Jacobs might try again later, but "her secretary was a very bad influence, and it must be stated that she must come alone to the next class, absolutely alone, or her instructors will refuse to tackle the case. Her temperament is bordering on hysteria. Either she is giggling or sour as a lemon." She showers her dog with a "sort of hysterical affection that might possibly have fear hidden behind it. If so, no dog would ever take her over."

Willi Ebeling outlined a long list of conditions Miss Jacobs would have to fulfill before she could be allowed to try again. Broadened to apply to all students, they reflect the shaping of Seeing Eye policy in the screening and preparation of applicants for future classes. Students must come alone. They must take their own dogs out to empty. They must have no social engagements during the turnover. They must be able to walk with a light touch on a human guide, not hanging on their arm. They must be prepared to accept mental and physical strain during the class. They must be genuinely fond of dogs and unafraid of them. They must be attentive to the instructor's words of explanation, must understand and remember them. Above all, they must be seeking a dog to win their own independence, not for the effect the dog may have on other people.

The failure of Sadie Jacobs sounded a discordant note on which to enter the new year, but 1929 had seen far more successes than failures. The school had held five classes, attempted seventeen turnovers, and graduated fourteen units working in nine states from coast to coast. It had won recognition by the Junior League, the Council of Jewish Women, the International Lions, and some workers for the blind. If it had alienated Herbert Immeln, it had gained a powerful friend in Mervyn Sinclair.

Best of all, it had gained experience from its failures. It would no longer seek to adapt trainers like Weber to its methods, but would form its own instructors. When cooperating with other organizations, it would insist on its own high standards of instruction and safety. Finally, it would be more selective in the acceptance of applicants to ensure that the case of Sadie Jacobs would not be repeated.

At four-thirty on the afternoon of March 26, Adelaide Clifford said goodbye to her mother in Grand Central Station and boarded a train for the West Coast. In crates in the baggage car were seven dogs she and Debetaz had trained in Morristown for an April 1 class in Berkeley. In May they

ON THE ROAD 103

would begin training a second string of dogs for a July class in San Francisco.

"Poor Mother must have been having fits," Adelaide recalled later. "I would be gone for four months. I was only nineteen, and my chaperone was a young Swiss who spoke hardly any English. At one thirty that morning, the porter woke me up with a wire that I was to get off the train at the next stop. Of course, I couldn't, so I went back to sleep, and Mother got over it."

For four days and nights, they crossed the country. At stops along the way, Debetaz and Adelaide let the dogs out to empty. In Cheyenne, one bitch ran away, and they held the train until she could be found, but they arrived in Berkeley with seven healthy dogs at last.

Dorothy Eustis was there to meet them. With Gretchen Green as her booking agent, she was winding up nearly three months of lectures and meetings from coast to coast. But Dorothy and Gretchen were bound East, so the reunion lasted only one evening. The class began in two days. The students were lodged in a hotel with Debetaz, while Adelaide took a room in a chaperoned dormitory at the University of California.

The arrangements had been many months in the making. Mrs. Eddy had begun soliciting interest in a class in the previous April. She had involved the local chapter of the Council of Jewish Women, and the American Foundation for the Blind had supplied Morris Frank with the names of local workers for the blind to contact. Robert Irwin and the American Foundation had also made it possible for Adelaide and Debetaz to get railroad tickets for half fare.

The class of seven was the largest yet enrolled, and its makeup differed from past classes. The 1929 graduates had included two doctors, two ministers, two agency executives, and a law student. The Berkeley students had humbler jobs. Miss Marie Ward was a dictaphone typist; Miss Mathilda

Allison, a clinical stenographer; Miss Ethel Roikjer, a violin teacher; and Miss Daisy O'Brien, a piano teacher. Mrs. Seeley was a housewife. Reginald White lived on his veteran's pension. Jack Stewart was a reed worker at Blindcraft, a sheltered workshop in San Francisco.

Blindcraft was run by the Mrs. Quinan who had refused Helen Keller permission to visit it, and at first she had objected that there was no room for a dog in her shop. Dorothy Eustis had made a convert of Mr. Roos, one of Blindcraft's most generous supporters, and under pressure Mrs. Quinan had not only capitulated, but permitted the enrollment of four additional workers from Blindcraft in the class scheduled for July.

The class began on time and progressed well with the exception of Mrs. Seeley, the housewife, who had too much residual vision to put complete confidence in her dog. Only one legally blind person in ten is totally blind. The blurred and distorted lights and shadows Mrs. Seeley "saw" confused her. Her consequent failure to follow her dog confused the dog as well. Her problem was never solved because she fell ill and had to drop out of the class.

For the first week they worked entirely in Berkely, but the streets were very quiet, and to expose the students to real traffic, they had to take them to San Francisco. The Bay Bridge had not yet been built. They took a ferry across the bay to the foot of Market Street, crossed San Francisco's version of "Death Street," and climbed the hill beside the clanging cable cars. Looking back, Adelaide wonders how she and Debetaz had the audacity to work new students through that chaos. "I don't know whether we were just young, stupid, crazy, or all three."

However, everything went "tic-tac." The turnover was completed, and two weeks later, Adelaide could report on the graduates. Debetaz had been up to Napa to check on Reginald White. "There is nowhere he won't go with his dog. Debetaz said he almost had heart failure watching him walk along the side of a cliff. Ethel Roikjer came to see me last night. She works tic-tac. She lives out of town and comes on a streetcar with her dog in one hand and her violin in the other. Miss Ward, I see off and on, works O.K. Miss O'Brien goes along the street like quicksilver."

Mathilda Allison belonged to a type that posed recurrent problems: the active, flamboyant, and frequently accomplished blind person who is too involved in other affairs to make the working of a dog an integral part of daily routine. She was campaigning for Governor Young. "She is all mixed up in politics and doesn't know whether she is going or coming. They tell me she never works her dog alone. If she doesn't work her pretty soon, it won't be much good to her."

Jack Stewart went home on schedule, and Adelaide sent the crate Mrs. Quinan had required to Blindcraft, but when Stewart and his dog showed up on Monday morning, "Some woman stopped him and told him he was cruel to his dog and that the harness he was using was inhuman. She had a policeman with her. Later on in the morning, a policeman appeared at Blindcraft and told Stewart he could not keep his dog in such a small crate. Mrs. Quinan was in the East Bay when all this happened," but Adelaide was sure "this was all nothing but a put up job."

On Wednesday, "Roos and I went to see Mrs. Quinan. We were there for two hours. Roos and Quinan did all the talking, and I never saw such sparks fly in my life. Of course, she denied that she had anything to do with the affair." The situation was still unresolved when Adelaide went off on vacation.

She had planned to take four days, "but I thought I'd better get back and see if the kennels were ready for the next load of dogs. Lucky I did. When I got there, nothing had been done." The preparation of these kennels had been covered in detail in correspondence. Willi Ebeling had written Morris the specifications the previous August, but apparently personality clashes between Mrs. Eddy, Miss Rosenfeld, executive of the Council of Jewish Women, and other local leaders had paralyzed initiative. Adelaide "couldn't make out what all the trouble was, but it finally came to the point that Debetaz and I built a fence around a barn and cleaned the place out. We worked two days and got it finished an hour before the dogs arrived. The new blind leaders, having been in crates for six days, looked more like pigs than dogs. They were a sight."

Unfortunately, they also made sound. They barked throughout the night. "There was an apartment house behind us, and they were the first to complain." The chief of police gave Adelaide a week to find a new place. "Mrs. Eddy couldn't seem to find anybody to help me, because all the club women for some reason were mad and were having some big club fight." Adelaide appealed to the mayor, the city manager, the Lions, and even the pound master, all to no avail.

"While all this was going on, Debetaz and I thought there must be a ringleader in the bunch that was doing all the barking. We decided on two dogs. Debetaz and I each took one. They didn't want to take the dog in the place I was living, but I finally got her in on condition that if she wet the rug, I would pay for it. At four o'clock in the morning she woke me up having puppies."

Debetaz was aroused from his sleep in the male sanctuary of the Y.M.C.A. by a frantic Adelaide. "She was yelling bloody murder! She had the bitch downstairs in a taxi having puppies. The driver was mad as a hornet."

There was worse to come. Adelaide's tale continued: "Some kind persons got it into their heads to poison the dogs, and poison the dogs they did. I had to get a vet, and one of the dogs almost passed out. Lucky I discovered what the matter was right away. The next day a policeman appeared at the kennel with a warrant for my arrest for violating the anti-noise ordinance."

There were some old houses on the Berkeley campus being demolished to make way for new construction. When she had freed herself of the law, Adelaide got out of her pants and into a dress and called on Mr. Nichols at the University. Using all the charm and eloquence she could muster, she finally persuaded him to give her an old house until July 1. "Debetaz and I built another fence out of nothing and cleaned the place out. It couldn't have been dirtier." It was Sunday, and they could find no one to help move the dogs, but they could not risk another complaint. They borrowed a wagon, piled the crates of ten dogs on top, and with Miss Adelaide Clifford, New York debutante, between the shafts and Debetaz pushing from behind, they moved from Berkeley to the university campus.

"Ina, one of the dogs Debetaz had with him at the Y.M.C.A., got hit by a car. Debetaz had her out for a run, and she ran across the street just as a car was coming around the corner." Physically, she was only grazed, "but she is so car shy, I can do nothing with her. Every time she sees a car coming down the street, she nearly goes crazy."

Since they had a total of ten dogs for a class of eight, the loss of Ina was not critical. Having survived puppies and poison, arrest and automobile accidents, constructing kennels and carting crates, Adelaide and Debetaz were eager for their real work and they had eight dogs ready for the July turnover. It opened on July 5, so as to avoid the problem of firecrackers. There were seven men and a woman: Ernest Blumenthal, A. Cunha, William Perkins, and Frank Klein worked at Blindcraft. Charles Brown and George Vahey were June graduates of the University of California and Stanford, respectively. John Jacobs and Miss Ollie Gish were unemployed. All eight were successfully turned over on July 27.

Ernest Blumenthal wrote,

> Yesterday was the last day of training for the class of which I was a member. It was a very delightful as well as an interesting and liberating experience. . . . With the guidance of Flou, I traveled home from the outlying districts of San Francisco on the streetcars, through the San Francisco ferry terminal, on the boat, and on the electric train to Oakland

and a considerable walk burdened with a suitcase before I reached home. Through this entire trip I touched only one person in what might be called a collision, when as I was walking with the crowd going aboard the ferry boat, I bumped a person with my suitcase, and that was the other person's fault. An hour after I arrived home, I walked several blocks to a carline, taking the streetcar and going to the Berkeley station to see Miss Clifford and Mr. Debetaz off on their way east. From Berkeley Station, I again took a streetcar and visited a friend in Berkeley, from where I walked home, a distance of two miles across several busy boulevards with which I was unfamiliar. It is in reality a realization of independence to go about in this manner after having been so restricted for twelve years.

Late in July, the scattered personnel of The Seeing Eye began to gather at Openaka. Adelaide and Debetaz boarded an eastbound train in Berkeley. Willi Ebeling, who had been to Europe to study technique at the Oldenburg school and Vevey, drove to New York to meet a new Swiss apprentice, Robert Chapellet, and ten trained dogs from L'Oeil Qui Voit. Adelaide took three months' vacation in Maine, but with the installation of Chapellet in the help house, the return of Debetaz, and the arrival of Jack Humphrey on August 1, Openaka began to hum.

Under Jack's supervision, Debetaz and Chapellet graduated a class of eight students in Morristown. Chappellet's salary was set at eighty dollars a month plus board and lodging. Debetaz's was raised to eighty-five dollars. In addition, there was an elaborate system of bonuses and penalties based on the rating each dog scored on the last blindfold test. A perfect score was 64, with both 63 and 64 considered "excellent," 61 and 62 "very good," and so on down the line.

On September 1, Morris arrived with Buddy. To test the use of a guide dog for the working blind and those in schools, he had spent a week in a sheltered workshop making brooms and two weeks in a school for the blind. Buddy had passed both tests with flying colors. After a few days conferring with Willi and Jack, Morris left for Washington.

In Washington, he was received at the White House by President Herbert Hoover. Morris exhibited Buddy's work and put her through obedience. She fetched the president's handkerchief for him once, but when she was immediately asked to do it again, she realized it was simply "busy work." She had been pleased to retrieve Morris's wallet for him on the *Tuscania*, but this was nonsense. She fetched the presidential handkerchief and, pinning it to the floor with her paw, deliberately tore it in two to the amusement of all concerned.

After this strictly ceremonial occasion, Morris got down to business in a meeting with General Hines and Captain Miller of the Veteran's Bureau. They were impressed by The Seeing Eye's nonprofit status and its turnover price of $300 per dog. Sinykin, it appeared, had been asking $1,000. However, there were no funds appropriated for the purchase of guide dogs. Morris suggested dogs could be paid for from the same funds used to buy artificial limbs, glass eyes, or other prosthetic devices. Hines and Miller seemed favorably disposed. They suggested circularizing the approximately 400 blind veterans with Seeing Eye literature.

Here Morris encountered the kind of ignorance of guide-dog technique that was to plague the school throughout its history. To the average American, a guide dog was a miracle, but it was an age of many miracles. The automobile was a miracle. Electricity was a miracle. Subways, airplanes, skyscrapers, and artificial ice cubes were miracles. The radio overtook the phonograph, and the talkies replaced silent films.

The guide dog was a biological, not a technological miracle. The proposed circularization of hundreds of blind veterans failed to take this into account. It implied that great numbers could be supplied simply by tooling up the assembly line to turn out guide dogs like Ford cars. The veterans could then be given a short course of instruction or possibly even a manual to teach them how to drive these marvelous canine machines.

Morris had to point out the complexities of the man-dog relationship. Establishing a harmony between one living organism and another was delicate and time-consuming. If even 200 veterans wanted guide dogs, it would take from four to five years to supply them all. Instead of mass circularization, he suggested that the government open its files to The Seeing Eye, so that the school could approach veterans selectively as dogs became available. The files were confidential, and opening them ran counter to normal procedure, but when Morris left Hines and Miller he felt that they might ultimately agree.

Meanwhile, the school's successes were offset by occasional failures. The ill-fated Birmingham class had to be canceled again, but with the aid of Mervyn Sinclair, Morris was able to line up a class in Pittsburgh. In September, two more students were graduated in Morristown, and in October, Philadelphia followed Nashville and San Francisco in opening its public transportation to guide dogs. Chapellet began a class of five in Morristown, and showed both courage and presence of mind on the night of October 13, when the Park Hotel, where he and the students were staying, caught fire. Under his supervision the dogs guided their masters to safety.

Two of these students proved special problems. Mr. Gilbert Newell of Greensboro, North Carolina, turned out to be a reformed alcoholic who reverted to drink under the nervous strain of the course and had to be hospitalized for several days. On his solemn pledge never to use the dog under the influence of alcohol, he was permitted to complete the turnover and did so successfully. Mr. Gordon Lathrop, a writer from New York, had a problem with too much vision compounded by another handicap: too much intellect or, rather, too much intellectual pride, the kind of intellect that insists on knowing with certainty. Knowing with certainty is impossible for a blind master. He must

leave the knowing to his dog and have the faith to trust
its judgment. By his failure to do this, Lathrop spoiled his
first dog and returned to New York without her. But he
planned to try again later.

After Jack Humprey's departure for Europe in November, Willi Ebeling began to notice careless work by the
new apprentice. He wrote Dorothy Eustis, "Had a bust with
Chapellet last night and almost sent him home. . . . I am
afraid he is a slacker, a man not to be trusted alone." On
the other hand, Adelaide, returned from Maine, was working very well. "If she continues as she is doing now, our
battles with her are over." Debetaz was "a man I can trust
anywhere. He has just finished nine dogs for the Pittsburgh
class: four excellent with 63 and 64 points, five very good,
all 62 points, just one below excellent. Beat that!"

In Pittsburgh, Debetaz would face the acid test. Of
course, he had been challenged earlier in Harrisburg, Berkeley, and San Francisco, but then the main responsibility
had fallen on Adelaide, and she had been there to translate
for him. Language, as he was first to admit, was his most
serious problem. He had made considerable progress in the
year since his arrival, but even after he had been in America
many years, one student wrote of him, "When I first came
to Morristown, I thought it odd that The Seeing Eye should
employ a man for such an important position who spoke
no English. I could never understand how all the students
managed to grasp what this man said. Then, one day, the
light dawned, and I realized he *was* speaking English."

His accent may have had the advantage of making
students listen more carefully, and his speech was enlivened
with many quaint "Debe-isms." With Gallic economy, he
telescoped "You would die laughing" and "You would laugh
yourself sick" into "You would die yourself sick," while a
gala party or "shindig" became a "shinding-dong." But for
all its color, Debetaz's manner of speaking was confusing,
and to have a language barrier on top of the other problems
in Pittsburgh compounded the challenge.

He had seven students he had never met, whom he must train on the wintry streets of a city he had never seen in a language he was still learning. He had to match dogs upset by a long journey in an unheated boxcar to the appropriate students, and he had to make his decisions as fast as he opened the crates. A November 30 letter gives some vivid glimpses into both his problems and his English.

"I arrive here yesterday morning with delay one hour, find two inches of snow, no dogs in station." At one in the afternoon, he located the dogs, but was told they could not be delivered. He went to the station, "chanced to find the right fellow, who put my dogs on truck and sent to Y.M.C.A. At four o'clock, start to give the dogs."

There were two students surnamed Douglas. Paul was white, Herbert was black. "The white one does not be strong for Babe, try to give Babe to Mr. Douglas black." The disorientation of the train trip was at once apparent. "Babe goes out from the crate and immediately jump on her new master and tries to bits him."

Debetaz instantly intervened, but not before the black Douglas had a scare, and his attempts to soothe the snappish Babe failed. Since Douglas lived in Pittsburgh, Debetaz put Babe in his room and sent Douglas home for the night. But he had his "other blinds" to think of.

He gave Night to the white Douglas, Billie to Mr. Altenhof, Fleury to Eugene Miller, Froelich to Mr. Burchfield, Peggy to Charles Cravats, and Lisa to Mr. Wilson, "man forty-three years old, look fine, don't say word." The reason for his ominous silence surfaced when he failed to show up in the dining room. Mr. Altenhof, his roommate, reported that Wilson was "mad and made his trunk to go home. I jump in his room, speak with that fellow for three quarters of an hour. He don't know himself for what he want leave, and after that, he comes again perfectly all right."

Debetaz had dinner with Wilson and took him to his room. "He told me I will see you in the morning, good night. That was eight and a half. At ten and a half, I have the phone from the Y.M.C.A. office saying he is gone and he leave his dog in his room."

Wilson may have been frightened by the incident with Babe, or he may have been temperamentally unsuited for a dog. Debetaz lamented, "I can't put this man on chain for keep him. I am myself very sorry because I see no reason why he can't have dog and make one nice piece of job. I will try today to give Lisa to the black Douglas and see what happens, because this man is now afraid about dogs." He shipped Babe and the empty crates back to Morristown. What had upset her remained a mystery. Any number of things could have happened when her crate was unattended, but she later recovered her good disposition and was turned over successfully.

Mr. Altenhof had physical problems. He was fifty-four, had been virtually chair-ridden since he went blind at the age of six, and "walk like if he is eighty years old, don't know nothing about walking alone, going down or up steps." He had to be carefully watched on the stairs and a few days of the lightest exercise made his feet and legs so painful that "in spite of all his willingness, he can't walk." The weather did not cooperate. "Yesterday rain. Today snow. What is coming for tomorrow?" Later, "Sidewalks and streets covered by coat of ice that don't help."

Debetaz was on twenty-four-hour call for all kinds of problems. If a dog emptied in her room, he cleaned up. He had to supervise trips up and down stairs from bedroom to dining room and out to the park for the dogs to empty. At meals, he helped his "blinds" to eat. If they had mail, he read it to them. If they had medical problems, he took them to the doctor.

This became necessary for Altenhof at the end of the second week. The doctor prescribed liniment and foot baths, which Debetaz administered, but the pain persisted. Altenhof walked too slowly to cross the street safely in traffic. At last, on Ebeling's advice, Altenhof was dropped from the class, and Billie was matched with Mr. Miller, who had been having difficulty with his first dog.

The class, which was scheduled to end before Christmas, lasted nearly to the new year, but the black Douglas overcame his fear of Lisa, and Debetaz had the thrill of turning over five men and dogs on his own.

Forty years later, Herbert, the black Douglas, wrote to him, "I am still able to walk about three miles every other day at the age of eighty-three years. I want to thank you for giving me the confidence to be independent and make a living and making it possible for my children to get a good education." His classmate, Paul, the white Douglas, who had gone through the University of Pittsburgh with Night, wrote at the same time. "To you, Mr. Debetaz, I owe all my forty years of pure happiness and perfect independence." But that was forty years later. As The Seeing Eye entered 1931, the evidence that its work would succeed was less conclusive.

CHAPTER 9

Home at Last

On the surface, 1930 had been a successful year. Dorothy Eustis's speaking tour with Gretchen Green had won new contacts and converts across the country. Mervyn Sinclair was an enthusiastic supporter at the Pennsylvania Council for the Blind, and Robert Irwin at the American Foundation had been extremely helpful. Morris had been received by President Hoover in the White House. Best of all, an instructor and two apprentices had graduated thirty-five dogs and humans, more than double the previous year's output. Yet Willi Ebeling had misgivings.

Debetaz had proven his worth as an instructor in Pittsburgh, but Willi had decided that Chapellet would not do. He was "too much the same type as Weber." Unless he was under direct supervision, he was prone to take unsafe shortcuts, and he would accept supervision only from Jack Humphrey. In December, Willi sent him back to Switzerland.

Adelaide too, was becoming slack in her habits. Her hours were irregular, and she stopped work on the streets of Morristown to gossip with friends. Her dogs were far behind schedule. In January, he redrew her contract. Two of her dogs were transferred to Debetaz. The deadline for the rest was extended to April 1, giving her five months to complete what was ordinarily done in three.

Eighteen dogs were now scheduled to be ready for a class in Washington on April 1. It was important to have eighteen blind students ready for them. Timing was crucial, because dogs could not be brought up to pitch and left in the kennels. They required the continuing challenge of work to keep from going sour. On January 1, Morris had sent out a letter and literature to a list of 700 prospects supplied by the Columbia Polytechnic Institute for the Blind. By March 1, there was not a single response of any kind.

Like Jack Humphrey, Willi Ebeling had a pragmatic and probing mind, but whereas Jack's restless imagination ranged over unexplored terrain, Willi's critical reason combed through previously plowed ground to make sure he knew what lay beneath every stone. He reexamined policies and procedures across the entire range of Seeing Eye activities. Dorothy saw clearly in black and white, and for this reason she could be—though very rarely—quite wrong, as when she told Morris that the job of managing director would "never take a man's whole time." Morris leapt to conclusions. For Willi, conclusions became hypotheses to be tested, then tested again. He was forever weighing and measuring, probing and sifting.

The character of his mind was reflected in his conversational style. It was punctuated with question marks. As he talked, an eyebrow lifted quizzically, and he queried his last remark with a "don't you know?" His "don't you knows" were like palpating antennae feeling out the mind of his listener and the terrain they were exploring.

He had serious doubts about the school's admission policy. Morris ought never to have accepted Altenhof in the Pittsburgh class. He could have proved to be another Sadie Jacobs. All candidates should be required to take a brisk hour's walk each morning and afternoon to get in trim. Fifty or fifty-five was probably the upper age limit for students. It was foolish to place dogs in situations where they were not wanted, such as at San Francisco's Blindcraft.

Willi had come into possession of a disturbing letter Kate Foley of Berkeley had written to a third party. Miss Foley had previously supported the school, but her letter stated that although the dogs cost $300 each, their owners in the Bay Area used them primarily for recreation. For the same price, she could have bought seven typewriters or eight radios that would have done more good for their blind owners than dogs and would have incurred no expense of upkeep.

Willi termed this "a vicious document, particularly coming from a professed admirer of the movement." In fact, it demonstrated a difference of professional perspective. Kate Foley taught braille. Johnny Jacobs, one of her students, stopped taking lessons as soon as he was accepted for a Seeing Eye class. His decision was illogical and no fault of The Seeing Eye, but Kate Foley may have concluded that the still unproven promise of a guide dog was seducing her students from learning a basic skill.

Disquieting news from graduates in the field upset Willi. In January, Reverend Seymour returned Ellin, who had become gun-shy. During a fall visit, Morris had analyzed the problem. Seymour must have corrected Ellin unjustly, following a loud noise of some kind, so that she had come to associate loud noises with her master's displeasure. Seymour, he said, had accepted this analysis at the time, but now tried to place all the blame on Ellin. Willi pronounced him "another minister who should be shoveling coal instead of preaching the gospel."

From Scranton he heard that Alberta Edwards' Iris had died only four months after graduation. The aunt in whose house she lived forced the dog to sleep in an unheated cellar during an Appalachian winter. Her callousness was in sharp contrast to the tenderness of a piano tuner in Florence, Italy, who left his dog at home when it rained and used his mother to guide him through the downpour.

Clyde Hutley wrote in great distress from upstate

New York. As in the previous winter, he had adopted the local practice of wearing "creepers," spiked metal frames clamped to his shoes for walking on ice. He had stepped on Sunny's paw and was unaware of it until a companion noticed the blood. He rushed her to a veterinarian, but she died the following day.

Edward Hoffman, who had graduated with Helga in August, was having difficulty in downtown Philadelphia. Helga, who had had exceptionally strong nerves, was now reluctant to work in traffic. Hoffman had been taught that a guide dog requires its master's undivided attention. Whenever walking with a friend, therefore, he should have known enough to put Helga on heel at short leash and use his friend as a guide. Instead, he had been working her in harness while chatting with a sighted companion. Witnesses had seen friends pulling Hoffman to the right while Helga was trying to lead him left in traffic. "No wonder she had difficulty!" Willi wrote, and of Hoffman's pretended ignorance, he exploded, "I have no patience with smart liars!"

To have a dog spoiled for any reason was saddening, but what especially gnawed at Willi Ebeling was his feeling that "we are getting the greatest backlash from what we considered our best students. The main blame for this, if it falls anywhere, goes right into training headquarters, and I include myself." He and the others had been certain of students at graduation who had had problems later. "Are we all fools here?" he asked. "They work alright when discharged, but the routine is not deeply enough embedded in the minds of the pupils that they will not vary from it. Perhaps one way we can protect ourselves a little is to take the full four weeks of the turnover, even if they finish sooner, as that extra time should make them firm in the routine. Perhaps we can draw up a form letter asking them, are you still doing this, that, or the other thing, enumerating the items they are apt to get careless on."

His uncertainty of the commitment of Dorothy Eustis underlay all his other misgivings. He wrote to ask her "what part America plays in your program? Is it a prime factor? Or is it going to become that?" He was anxious, because in addition to her work with French, Italian, and Swiss blind, Dorothy was now beginning to excite interest in England. Making a new start in England when the American movement was still so precarious ran counter to his conservatism. "You have Italy, Switzerland, France, America and also England to cover. If help is needed, you have one man to send. If all the babies should cry at the same time, Jack has to be divided into fifths, and as science has not yet given us a practical solution for such division, you will have neither five fifths, nor one."

Yet despite his many doubts and uncertainties, Willi Ebeling had an unshakeable faith in dogs, both as physical and as emotional guides. Gilbert Newell was an alcoholic, but he loved Hebe, and he had promised never to work her under the influence of liquor. If he loved her enough, that love would bring him through and keep him to his promise. Gordon Lathrop had been a most difficult student. After his first failure, he had returned to Morristown a second time. It took a total of twelve weeks and two spoiled dogs to achieve a successful working unit. Never mind. He would have invested more time, more of himself, another dog, and still considered it worth the price. Willi sympathized with Clyde Hutley for the loss of Sunny and rejoiced in his turnover with Babe, who had recovered from her emotional upset in Pittsburgh. They performed "some of the finest traffic work I have ever seen." From irritation with Hoffman, he became all patience, carefully explaining his past errors and rejoicing in his new understanding.

Willi and Adelaide had been on a collision course for weeks, and late in February the clash came. A stormy scene ended in Adelaide's resignation. Afterwards, Willi blamed himself for losing his temper, and it is regrettable that they parted on bad terms, but Adelaide's ultimate departure was inevitable. Even under Jack, of whom she was far fonder than Willi, she would have realized that she had neither the physical strength nor the dedication to devote her whole life to guide dogs.

Adelaide's work had been vital during The Seeing Eye's first two years. Of the fifty dogs turned over, she had been partially or wholly responsible for more than half, and she had been the only qualified instructor for a crucial fourteen months. Dorothy Eustis did not exaggerate when she inscribed a Seeing Eye booklet "To Adelaide, without whom The Seeing Eye would not exist."

Adelaide was sorely missed. Debetaz alone was responsible for a Washington class that might have as many as fifteen applicants. Illness among his dogs had set their work back, and Adelaide's string was below par. There was no recourse but for Willi to pitch in. At forty-nine he found it a strain. "Gosh, I'm sore," he wrote Jack. "I can hardly waddle."

But what bothered him most was Dorothy's commitment in England. The United Kingdom insisted on six months' quarantine for any dog that entered, so it was impossible to train dogs in Vevey and ship them to England for an immediate turnover. An instructor would have to be sent to train a string of English dogs from the ground up. With the exception of Jack, there was no one in Vevey who could do the job. It fell therefore to G. William Debetaz, as he now called himself. Dorothy decreed he would sail for Europe right after the Washington turnover and would not return until November. He would be lost to The Seeing Eye for nearly six months.

Willi took consolation where he could. "Hutley writes that he is just plain tickled pink with his new dog. He says, 'I am really stuck on this dog. She really has the goods.' Well, we had a devil of a time to convince him, but he is getting there now. Babe, you know, is just the opposite from Sunny. A year ago, no other dog but Sunny would have done the trick. You should see the difference in Clyde today compared with when he came for his first dog. He impresses one as changed from poverty to prosperity. Delightful!"

There were other paeans from the field. Ann Connelly had used her new freedom to leave the Vermont Association for the Blind and start a gift shop, traveling to take orders for her wares. "Betty helps me to cover the ground rapidly. I can take her on any bus in the State of Vermont or the Central Vermont Railroad. I can take her to all hotels and to other public places. In my new work, I find her a great help, not only as a guide, but as an attraction as well. People admit me and buy my wares many times to see Betty."

Dr. Harris and Tartar had also taken to travel. "Tartar is working beautifully, and I go about wherever and whenever I fancy. I have just returned from a trip through northern Georgia with the finest four-legged guide in the whole wide world, even including Buddy. Tartar works in Athens, Atlanta, Augusta, and Macon as accurately and safely as she works in Savannah. In hotels and on the street, I have no difficulty."

Such reports justified and fortified Willi Ebeling's faith in guide dogs, but they could not obliterate his awareness of serious weaknesses in The Seeing Eye, and he looked forward to Dorothy Eustis's arrival from Switzerland with a mixture of hope and dread.

The World Conference and the meeting of the American Association of Workers for the Blind were scheduled consecutively in Washington, D.C., in May. Dorothy reported to both on the use of the guide dog as a leader for the blind.

She began with a brief history of the guide dog, dating back to the writings of Father Johann Klein in Vienna in 1819. She sketched in the origins and development of the guide-dog movement in Germany, noting that there were an estimated 4,000 units functioning there today. She explained how her *Saturday Evening Post* article had brought

Morris Frank to her attention and how this had led to the founding of both The Seeing Eye and L'Oeil Qui Voit.

Her commanding presence and clear sensible exposition held her audience from the beginning, and her subsequent remarks made some telling points. Instead of shrugging off difficulties, Dorothy emphasized them. Capable instructors were extremely rare. It was a case of "many are called, but few are chosen." Dogs had to be taught to disobey intelligently. She explained the criteria for the selection of suitable dogs and stressed the crucial importance of the three or four weeks' course to match the dogs to human masters. She cited the percentages of dogs who failed in preliminary training (2 to 4 percent), who failed during the turnover (5 percent), and who failed following their return home with their masters (3 percent). In most cases, failures at home were owing to misuse by the masters.

She asked, "If we do actually know that some masters misuse their dogs, why do we not make a more careful selection of masters?" In answer, she admitted, "No school has yet evolved any method of examination by which they can tell which blind will make good with their guide dogs and which will fail. The records of every school are filled with cases of seemingly perfect students who failed and seemingly impossible students who have made good."

She stated her conviction that guide dogs should not be placed with all blind persons. Home or working conditions would frequently render a dog impractical. Since an instructor working full-time could only turn out between twenty and twenty-five dogs a year, only those who had prospects of real benefit from the use of a dog should be considered. Dorothy went on to describe what the benefits for this limited number were in terms of improved earnings, improved health, and improved peace of mind, but she avoided making exaggerated claims. She concluded with grateful thanks "to those organizations who have and are lending us their aid and experience."

Willi wrote Jack, "Dorothy went over big. Her speech

earned the greatest applause of the entire lot. Sinclair, Morris, and Mrs. Patchen with their dogs were a beautiful sight and certainly created a sensation." An incidental dividend was a report that Blindcraft in San Francisco was now wholly reconciled to workers having dogs. Willi exulted, "Smoke that one! Dandy! Just as soothing as your snuff."

But the basic reason for Willi's exuberance was Dorothy's renewed commitment to the American school. She was prepared for an aggressive new program which she would finance from her own pocket.

To begin with, she proposed closing the Nashville office from August 1 to March 1. Instead of trying to line up classes by mail in various parts of the country, Morris would focus on Pennsylvania, New York, and New Jersey. With a car and a driver, he would travel extensively through these states, studying local conditions, giving talks, and interviewing agency heads and blind candidates in person.

When Mrs. Eustis first unveiled this scheme to Morris, he was less than enchanted. "Suppose I'd rather stay in Nashville," he asked.

"In that case, Morris," she replied calmly, "there will be no Seeing Eye." Morris struck his colors.

But that was only the beginning. Willi wrote Jack, "We are now out to find a house in Morristown for the blind and, if possible, something that will permit shifting of training headquarters under one roof." It was a good time to buy, because "Everything is topnotch rotten."

Dorothy's willingness to spend money decisively was basic to success. The Seeing Eye was not wasteful. To save paper, Willi Ebeling put carbon copies of his correspondence on both sides of the page. Instructors made their own leashes. But Dorothy saw to it that the school did not have to compromise its high standards for financial reasons.

The acquisition of a house in Morristown would mean a sweeping reorganization of The Seeing Eye. Headquarters would be permanently moved from Nashville. The kennels would be shifted from Openaka. Students could be housed in the school's own facilities, so that all operations could be centralized. Morris would be relieved of the administrative duties for which he had neither the taste nor the training. His major work would be in the field. Willi Ebeling would take over finance and administration, supervise training, and correspond with blind graduates on their problems.

In the interim, there was much work to be done. In Philadelphia, Dorothy approached officials of the Pennsylvania Railroad to get permission for guide dogs to travel on passenger cars. Although it was not finally confirmed until October 15, the railroad agreed that dog owners with permits issued by the American Foundation for the Blind could ride with their dogs in its cars.

After graduating a class of seven students in Washington in May, Debetaz sailed for Europe to prepare the first string of guide dogs in England. Willi Ebeling followed a few days later for further study at the German schools and at L'Oeil Qui Voit. He hoped also to hire an instructor from the Oldenburg school, which was about to close down.

In New York on her way back to Switzerland, Dorothy employed as Morris's driver and secretary a young woman recommended by Gretchen Green, Marie MacKee. As Morris was winding up his affairs and insurance business in Nashville, he was commissioned a colonel on the staff of the governor of Tennessee "in recognition of his signal contribution to the rehabilitation of the blind." On August 1, in a new car with a new secretary, Colonel Morris S. Frank and Buddy set off on a trip to explore and improve the opportunities for guide dogs in New York, New Jersey, and Pennsylvania.

Toward the end of August, a letter from Dorothy in Vevey informed him that she had taken two further steps. "I have arranged to buy the Schneider property on Whippany Road for The Seeing Eye. I shall try to hold it until such time as the organization can afford to buy it from me at the price I paid for it plus interest." For fifty acres, a

main house, a gate house, and several outbuildings, she
had agreed to pay $30,000. She also planned to speed the
time when the school could afford to buy it from her. She
was negotiating with a young woman to help her organize
a finance committee and raise funds when she returned to
the States in 1932. Such a program was needed to buttress
the personal philanthropy of Dorothy and a handful of her
family and friends.

Morris and Mervyn Sinclair worked out a comprehensive schedule for blanketing the Commonwealth of Pennsylvania with lectures and interviews. They estimated that the
state had a potential of 600 guide-dog users. Morris asked
Dorothy, "How many instructors will you be sending me?"
When he learned that none were available, he confined re-
cruitment to a class to be held in Morristown in November,
when Debetaz would return from England. In January,
Debetaz would entrain for Kansas City. A wealthy local
industrialist and shepherd breeder, R. L. Grey, had offered
to provide both the dogs and financial support for a class
there. Since Debetaz must train the dogs before the class,
he would be away for four months.

Morris drove through Pennsylvania giving talks and
interviews. He was not happy with Mrs. MacKee. Apparently, she thought of herself as his manager and impresario,
rather than as his secretary and chauffeur. When Willi
Ebeling returned from Europe in October, Mervyn Sinclair
confided that Marie MacKee "did not know what it was all
about."

Willi immediately took charge of many details on the
purchase of the Schneider estate. He had the title searched
and negotiated the tentative resale of twenty acres. He received shipments of furniture Dorothy had sent from her
house on the Main Line and her New York apartment. On
November 10, he reported to Dorothy, "The first load of
furniture arrived today. How swell the home is going to
be! Really too fine for the purpose!"

He took out fire and theft insurance, installed fire

extinguishers, and sent his handyman to pick up some furnishings contributed by the Alfred Kays, friends of Gretchen's. He was at the steamer to meet Debetaz with ten Fortunate Fields dogs for the next class. It would open on November 23 in the Washington Hotel in Morristown. Dorothy was reassured that Willi's hand was on the tiller, but there was an ominous passage in his last letter:

"Now to something less pleasant. Frankness, I think, is in order." The depressed state of the stock market had caught up with him at last. He and Florence must sharply reduce their style of living. "What I probably shall have to decide on is to go to Europe and remain with my mother until the financial sky shows a brighter face." The move, if it came, would not be until March or April, but it threatened a serious loss to the school.

On November 30, Dorothy received a transatlantic phone call. She was in Paris to watch the turnover of five dogs to Frenchmen under Jack Humphrey and Missy Doudge. Willi Ebeling was on the other end of the wire. He reported that the local zoning board was planning to ban the use of the Schneider estate for a guide-dog school. It would meet December 2. Although there were only forty-eight hours in which to act, and the school had a large class of students in progress, they agreed on a bold stroke. Willi would move the class into the building to establish residence, so that the school could not be excluded after the fact.

It was a prodigious undertaking. The house was without heat, light, telephone, or water. Some of the pipes were frozen and had to be fixed. Supplies must be bought, and furniture arranged. But they managed it. Willi wrote, "We moved heaven and earth and moved ourselves into the home and had our first supper there Tuesday night, fourteen at the table." Morris described it as "the realization of our dream to be at the head of the table with eight blind people and eight bright-eyed dogs under the table." The threat of exclusion was nullified.

The class was presenting problems. Willi and Debetaz

found that the dogs brought over from Vevey had "but little idea about traffic." After two weeks, Willi tested Ann Connelly, back for a replacement, and reported she could have been killed three times. He and Debetaz would have to work all students singly, rather than in pairs, in order to give them special attention.

On Sunday, December 6, Morris phoned to say that the car in which he and Marie MacKee had been driving to Pittsburgh had turned over twice and come within six inches of plunging down a 2,000-foot precipice. Although Morris and Mrs. MacKee were only bruised, Buddy suffered two cuts, and Morris was disinclined to accept a blowout as the cause of the accident. A couple of days later, when Marie MacKee neglected to inform him of a speaking date, they came to a shouting match. "Uncle Willi," as Morris was now calling him, agreed to let her contract terminate at the end of December.

The class ended before Christmas. The difficulty with traffic was owing to the decline of tourism in Switzerland. Thanks to the Depression, the dogs had dealt with very few cars prior to their arrival in America. Even so, seven students graduated, and the two who did not owed their failure to their own defects, not to any fault of the dogs. The head of the Allentown workshop, which sent three students, wrote Willi Ebeling on December 28, "The performance of these dogs has amazed our community. Thousands who have seen the dogs leading their blind masters through the crowded streets during these busy Christmas shopping days stand and watch in awe. They wonder, no doubt, who could have trained men and dogs to work together so perfectly."

Willi took satisfaction in the fact that the class had cost $260 less in the new home than it would have in the hotel, and he was feeling less pessimistic about remaining in the States. Florence Ebeling had always had servants, but she found she rather liked doing without them; and living with her German mother-in-law was not an attractive alternative. Jack wrote Willi, "You have made The Seeing

Eye what it is in the States. For goodness sake, try to think of some way to stay."

Dorothy Eustis arrived on February 14, and it was she who thought of a way for him to stay. She brought him onto the school staff at a modest salary. She also set about reincorporating the school in New Jersey. The incorporators were Dorothy Eustis, her eighteen-year-old son Harrison, Morris Frank, and the Ebelings. For trustees, she added her brother, Harry Harrison, and replaced Florence Ebeling with a local shepherd breeder and old friend of Willi's, Charlie Baiter. The officers were Dorothy Eustis, president; her brother, vice president; Jack Humphrey, vice president, division of training and research; Morris Frank, vice president, division for the blind; and Willi Ebeling, secretary-treasurer.

Four years before, Dorothy had urged Morris to choose a board of trustees as representative as possible. Now that she had decided to assume full responsibility for The Seeing Eye, she chose a board of only six, including three members of her family and two members of her paid staff, with another member of her staff as the third vice president. If there is irony in this, it is nevertheless true that with the purchase of the house in Morristown and the new assignment of roles, she had arrived at the basic working formula that would guide the destinies of the school over the course of the next decade.

The Five Founders (*clockwise*): Dorothy Eustis supplied the vision; Jack Humphrey, the training genius; Willi Ebeling, the managerial skill; and Morris and Buddy, the pioneering courage to blaze the trail.

A 1465 woodcut shows the old model—"a cur dragging a blind man at the end of a string."

Jack Humphrey follows a blind student and dog training at L'Oeil Qui Voit in Vevey.

Hans von Saarbrücken, the dog who inspired the breeding program of Fortunate Fields.

Dorothy and George Eustis teach obedience on the grounds of their Swiss chalet.

Morris and Buddy show a new model of man and dog to admirers on the streets of Vevey.

Mrs. Elford Eddy and Beda training in Nashville in 1929.

Jack Humphrey and Alexander Woollcott, the radio voice of The Seeing Eye.

"Debby" Debetaz works a dog onto
the Morristown bus.

A class of students works down the
drive in Whippany to take the bus
to Morristown.

Dog in training learns to avoid barrier slapped by instructor. Another dog is taught the same lesson with an overhanging branch. Instructor points out a curb with hand and stamping foot.

Two instructors take test under blindfold as supervisor scores their work. Inset shows rigid harness handle, an advance over flexible loops. Dog steers blindfolded instructor between wall and sign.

Aerial photograph of the new school and grounds overlooking the Washington Valley.

Seeing Eye dogs have brought their masters new freedom—in jobs, transportation, public acceptance.

BOOK III

Maturity by Design

CHAPTER 10

Philosophy
at Openaka

ON A JUNE morning in 1933, Willi Ebeling herded four houseguests at Openaka into his big Packard to drive them to the meeting of the American Association of Workers for the Blind in Richmond. They were C. L. Broun of the New York State Commission for the Blind, Mary Dranga Campbell of the Brooklyn Board of Charities, Mervyn Sinclair of the Pennsylvania Council for the Blind, with his dog Kara, and Elizabeth Hutchinson, his assistant. They were all good friends by now, but as he drove south, it occurred to Willi Ebeling that the single thread that had drawn them all together was a common interest in Morris Frank. In fact, bringing these four to Openaka may have been one of Morris's most important services to the guide dog movement, because they played a critical role in shaping its philosophy.

Like Sinclair, C. L. Broun had been a successful businessman until he went blind. Director of placement for the New York State Commission for the Blind, he was a native of Virginia who had never lost the courtly manners of the Southern gentleman. He was too old to get a dog himself, but he was a believer in the movement.

Mary Dranga was one of the first workers for the blind with a graduate degree in social work, and was widely respected in the field. When her sister died in 1911, she had moved in with her widowed brother-in-law, Charles Campbell, to look after his three children. They were married the following year, and professionally they made an effective team. Mary was co-editor with Charlie of *Outlook for the Blind*, and assistant superintendent of the Ohio School for the Blind. Temperamentally they were mismatched. Charlie was a born extravert, all charm, wit, and diplomacy. Mary kept her emotions hidden behind an imposing Viking exterior. She was a no-nonsense professional who could be devastatingly frank. Inevitably, their marriage broke up. After the war, Mary spent three years working in child welfare in Serbia. She preceded Sinclair as head of the Pennsylvania Council and went from there to the Missouri State Commission for the Blind and later to the Brooklyn Board of Charities. She had befriended Morris in Wawasee in 1929.

Mervyn Sinclair had been a "true believer" in The Seeing Eye ever since acquiring Kara in December 1929. Kara had had a role in enlisting the fourth member of the party, Elizabeth Hutchinson. A well-bred and extremely attractive Philadelphian in her twenties, Ibby had spent some years as occupational therapist for the Visiting Nurse Service when a friend suggested she might like to work for Sinclair. She recoiled sharply. She wanted nothing to do with "The Blind" and would have refused to meet Sinclair if a luncheon date had not already been arranged. She was waiting for him at the appointed restaurant "when the elevator door opened and out came this tall, handsome, very distinguished looking gentleman with a perfectly gorgeous dog." In that split second, Mervyn Sinclair and Kara shattered her stereotyped image of "The Blind Man," and Ibby Hutchinson went to work for the council.

In her new job, she was asked to drive Morris and Buddy on visits to Pennsylvania agencies. "Morris could be perfectly awful!" she recalls. At lunch in a restaurant, she offered to pour cream in his coffee "the way I would have for anyone. I wasn't even thinking about his being blind. He almost took my head off. 'I can pour my own cream!' That's the way he was." She laughs. "People either liked Morris, or they didn't. I liked him."

The four were frequent weekend visitors to Openaka. Morris was such a regular that he referred to Florence Ebeling as "my Northern mother." Dorothy Eustis and the Humphreys represented a different element of the Openaka weekends. Like Willi Ebeling, Dorothy and Jack were primarily "dog people" with no expertise on blindness. Broun, Mary Campbell, Mervyn Sinclair, and Ibby Hutchinson had backgrounds in work for the blind. They were "blind people." The weekends at Openaka brought the "dog people" and the "blind people" together.

In conversations that lasted far into the night, the two groups gradually fused their ideas. Over a period of several years, they shaped what was fundamentally a new philosophy of work with the blind. *With* the blind, not *for* the blind. Morris insists that no one person can be given more credit than another for this philosophy. Openaka offered the ambiance, and the Ebelings' hospitality was the catalyst, but all made their individual contributions.

Certain fundamentals had already been established. Happily, The Seeing Eye did not include the condescending phrase, "for the blind," in its title. Moreover, it had been consciously conceived, not as a charity, but as a service to provide guide dogs for deserving blind people at cost. The distinction between a charity and a service at cost is philosophically and psychologically vast, but the school's financial policy became a philosophy only after some trial and error.

From the first, students of means had been expected to pay for their dogs. Others were asked to contribute what they could to the revolving fund out of the increased earnings their dogs would make possible. In the early years the estimated cost of a dog fluctuated between $170 and $375. Since most blind people at that time would have found even the lower figure beyond their means, the school encouraged the granting of scholarships by individuals, clubs, or groups. The final selection of applicants was reserved to the school, but donors could nominate candidates of their own choosing, and at first they were permitted to know who had received their scholarships. Unfortunately, one service club became so self-congratulatory of its own generosity that it continually reminded both the community and the recipient who had paid for his Seeing Eye dog. He was expected to repay the club, not only with his gratitude, but with the donation of his services as a professional piano player at the club's social functions. He felt his situation thoroughly humiliating, and to prevent any recurrence with other graduates, the school kept the identities of all future scholarship recipients in strictest confidence.

As the school's financial position improved, the practical need for student payments decreased, but The Seeing Eye continued to ask its students to assume some financial obligation for their dogs. Morris did not want students to "look upon our work as something due them and accept it in the same spirit as favors received from other blind organizations." In 1933, a new contract requiring a student to pay $300 for a dog specified that the actual cost was "at least twice the price quoted." In 1934, the amount to be paid was reduced to $150. As Ibby Hutchinson put it, "No individual or organization can relieve the student of this obligation, for if he is unwilling to accept it, he is apt to be unsuccessful with a Seeing Eye dog." Willi Ebeling was more affirmative: "Blind people have for centuries been prime objects of charity. They have many of them become used to the idea that people give things to them, and they have therefore relaxed their own efforts to do things for themselves. When a student undertakes to repay $150 for his dog, more often than not he is for the first time recognizing his capacity to do something for himself."

This was a revolutionary concept among workers for the blind in that day, and it took some time for "the dog people" and "the blind people" to agree that it was good for blind students to be challenged. It represented a sharp break with tradition.

In 1929, Edward Allen proposed the following examination question for his Harvard students: "Comment on the statement, 'What the public thinks the blind are, that they tend to become.' " Forty years later, Robert Scott, a Princeton sociology professor, might have rephrased it: "What agencies for the blind think the blind are, that they will become." Scott wrote a controversial book, *The Making of Blind Men*. It suggested that agencies for the blind tended to make people blind, make them blinder than they really were by forcing them to conform to the stereotype of helplessness that justified the existence of the agencies. The message they conveyed to their clients was "Be helpless, so that we can help you."

The above may be a distortion of Scott's thesis and an overstatement of the facts, but it is certain that many agencies for the blind both then and much later tended to project an unfortunate stereotype of blindness and to force it on their clients. As late as 1960, a nationally-known and highly reputable agency sent out an appeal for funds that created the acronym BLINDNESS from the first letters of Bewilderment, Loneliness, Insecurity, Neglect, Dependency, Nostalgia, Emptiness, and Sedentary Solitude. At about the same time, an equally well-known agency rebuked a volunteer for having taken several of its blind clients out for an evening that included cocktails, dinner, and a musical comedy, all at his own expense. He was accused, he said, of putting dangerous ideas into their heads. They might forget that they were supposed to be Bewildered, Lonely, Insecure, Neglected, and Dependent.

Seeing Eye students were not expected to languish in Sedentary Solitude, and they were challenged by more than the obligation to pay for their dogs. The ownership of a dog was itself a challenge beyond anything that blind Americans had experienced before. Dorothy, Jack, and Willi, the "dog people," looked at the man-dog equation from the canine point of view. They might have rephrased Edward Allen's statement to "What a guide dog needs his blind master to be, that he *must* become!" There was no alternative. An educated guide dog was far too precious to waste on a human who was unwilling or unable to meet the demands of ownership.

Working a dog required strength, coordination, and orientation. The dogs walked fast and must be worked two or three miles a day, if they were not to grow stale and unsafe. Generally, people over fifty-five could not meet the physical strain of a first dog, although those who kept in trim with dogs were able to train with new dogs into their eighties. Adolescents under sixteen tended to lack the sense of responsibility that ownership of a dog required.

A master must have the courage to trust his dog's judgment, or it would stop working. There was need for moral courage, too. Newell had shown it in keeping his pledge not to touch alcohol, but Alberta Edwards had lacked the backbone to refuse her aunt's demand that Iris sleep in a cold cellar. Hedrick had submitted meekly to his landlord's prohibition, "No dogs allowed."

It was the duty of all Seeing Eye graduates to get their dogs received in public places. They owed it to themselves and to those who would come after them. If dogs were to be received, they must be made to behave. This imposed the far more difficult task of making the public behave. Having taught his dog to lie quietly at his feet underneath the table in a restaurant, her master must then teach the waiters and the other guests not to tempt her to misbehave by patting, talking to her, or offering her food.

Since the challenges of ownership were so great, it was obvious that guide dogs were not for everyone, but as Dorothy had told the World Conference and the A.A.W.B., it was very difficult to tell who would succeed and who would fail. At Openaka, the "dog people" and the "blind people" gradually came to agree on screening procedures, but not until Sinclair had disputed one of the criteria for admission. The Seeing Eye had adopted without testing the European belief that a dog should not be paired with anyone who had been blind for less than two years, on the theory that it took at least that long "to learn to be blind." Sinclair persuaded Willi Ebeling to accept three newly blind students in the same class with others of long standing. The newly blind learned faster than the others. They had a fresher recollection of their freedom, were more eager to regain it, and had had a shorter time to sink into habits of dependency. Thereafter, The Seeing Eye gave priority to the newly blind.

The "blind people" assisted in the admission process. Both Mary Campbell and Ibby Hutchinson interviewed applicants. In a swing through Albany, Rochester, and Buffalo, Broun and Morris personally screened seventy-nine of the most promising candidates culled from the New York State Commission files. From complaints she had heard from graduates, Ibby Hutchinson was persuaded that the school's teaching methods put too much emphasis on the dog and made too little provision for individual differences in the students. She was invited to spend a month with a class in May of 1933 as an observer. The experience changed her mind.

In the end, the "dog people" and the "blind people" arrived at a consensus that projected a new goal for The Seeing Eye. Other agencies taught their clients to be blind. Seeing Eye students would be taught to be as normal as possible. The dogs would give their masters the freedom to move into the sighted world. For this reason, The Seeing Eye made the fewest possible concessions to its students' blindness.

Headquarters had been a family dwelling and retained a homelike atmosphere. The students slept not in dormitories, but in bedrooms on the upper floors. Since the staircase to the second floor had two landings and twenty steps, it offered plenty of practice in going up and down stairs. The living room was comfortably arranged with Dorothy's own furniture. In the dining room, students, staff, and visitors sat at a large family table. The men were asked to wear coats and ties and the women, skirts or dresses for lunch and dinner. They were addressed as Mr., Mrs., or Miss, and they were expected to cut their own meat and butter their own bread. In other words, they were treated like ladies and gentlemen and asked to dress and behave like ladies and gentlemen.

For those from families or institutions that had taught them to be blind, this was a challenge. Many had scanty ideas of table manners. One young woman of twenty-three, brought up in a foundling home, had never used a knife, fork, or spoon. She ate with her fingers. Others had never been to the hairdresser and had no idea of cosmetics. Where blind people were seen only by their families or were segregated with other blind people, their appearance did not matter. The Seeing Eye wanted its graduates out in the world.

The school could not attempt a total rehabilitation, but it could give some preparation for life in the outside world. To assist in this process, Mary Campbell was hired as executive secretary of the division of the blind in October 1934. Just a year later, Ibby Hutchinson became her assistant. If a student could not handle a knife and fork, he was given a private lesson. Ibby Hutchinson showed women how to apply cosmetics or suggested an appointment with the hairdresser. There were many subtle ways in which students were helped to understand what it meant to be part of a seeing world. Perhaps I can best illustrate from my own experience.

When I first arrived at The Seeing Eye, I was twenty-one and had been blind for six months. My mother drove me to Morristown, and we were met in the driveway by my instructor, Mr. Northrup. Following his instructions, interspersed with many asides to my mother ("Let him do it himself, Mrs. Putnam"), I carried my bag up the stairs to my bedroom, was shown the position of my bed, bureau, and closet, and was then left with my mother in the recreation room. After a cigarette and a parting conversation, I went down with my mother to say goodbye on the front porch. Back in the house, I crossed the hall and was groping for the banister of the staircase, when I heard Mr. Northrup call from the landing.

"Keep your head up, Mr. Putnam," he said, "and stand straight."

At once I realized that my neck was sticking forward apelike in my uncertainy.

"I'm sorry," I said foolishly.

"It's a frequent mannerism of the new blind," Mr. Northrup answered, "but it's a good thing to catch early."

Within fifteen minutes of my arrival at The Seeing Eye, I had my first lesson in personal appearance in a sighted world. Two weeks later, Miss Hutchinson was reading me a letter from a college girl who invited me for a weekend at a ski resort. I commented on the absurdity of myself on skis.

"I don't know," Miss Hutchinson said, "maybe you ought to try it."

I had never been on skis before I was blind, but as it turned out, I did take up skiing that winter and have enjoyed it ever since. Perhaps, at least in part, I owe it to Elizabeth Hutchinson's having shaken my incredulity that morning.

Another student arriving at the school for the first time had much the same experience as I with Mr. Northrup, but having been blind much longer and sheltered by an overprotective family, he had become what Morris Frank called "blind-minded." He was flabbergasted when the staff member who greeted him told him to pick up his bag and follow him. The staff member talked him upstairs, pounded out the position of bed, bureau, and closet, and advised him to unpack. This was too much for the young man.

"In case you haven't noticed," he blurted, "I am blind."

"So am I," Morris Frank answered, "but I never let it interfere with my appetite, and dinner is in twenty minutes. Better get yourself unpacked."

Morris often resorted to such shock tactics to stiffen the spines of the "blind-minded," but the message was clear, and it was startlingly different from that of most agencies for the blind. Instead of "Be helpless, so that we can help you," it was "Help yourself, or nobody can help you."

CHAPTER 11

The Power
of Light

HARKING BACK to a spring morning in 1932, Margaret Kibbee recalls, "I was at the reception desk when Mrs. Eustis came into the office and announced, 'I have been told that Mr. Harold Strong is the finest fund-raising man in New York, and I would like to see him.' She was a rather small woman, crisp and very direct in her manner, and with a humorous gleam in her eye. The best word I can think of to describe her is perky. I remember we smiled at one another when I told her I would tell him she was there."

That marked the beginning of one of the most remarkable fund-raising successes in history. With the deepening Depression, the increased expenses of the Whippany house, the expanding payroll, and her other commitments, Dorothy was finding her resources strained. Charlie Baiter, the new trustee, expressed misgivings at the school's dependence on the personal philanthropy of Mrs. Eustis and a few supporters. The death or disaffection of any one of them could cripple The Seeing Eye's program. It would be far sounder to build up a broad base of small contributions. A friend of Gretchen Green's recommended Harold Strong to Dorothy Eustis.

She liked the Strong company from the beginning. It

was young, energetic, and highly organized. Although it would grow much larger there were only four on the staff at the time: Strong, Dickson Hartwell, Margaret Kibbee, and a secretary. Dorothy worked with them on a personal basis.

Their first task, says Margaret Kibbee, "was to set up a good solid sponsoring group made up of men and women who were dependable, highly respected, known for integrity, influential, and with access to other people of the same type. I remember Mr. Strong and Mrs. Eustis spending days going over lists of people, the *Social Register*, club membership lists, etc., and discussing them before settling on Herbert Satterlee as their first choice. They then discussed how to approach him, what program they would present to him, and how to present it. Mrs. Eustis was enthusiastic, vitally interested, and eager. She was full of ideas of her own and contributed a great deal to the plan."

Satterlee was a well-known New York lawyer, a brother-in-law of J. P. Morgan, and just the sort of person whose reputation for integrity would give the right tone to the committee. He was also hard to reach, but Dorothy was patient and persistent. It took her three separate interviews to persuade him to give a luncheon for a group of influential friends at the Downtown Association. Morris showed films, and Dorothy spoke. No one was asked for money. The program was so well received that Satterlee gave a second luncheon. A few members were added to the committee, but the recruiting process was highly selective, and it took time.

According to Margaret Kibbee, Gretchen Green was invaluable. "Her sense of humor was tremendous, and she knew how to use it to amuse and catch one's attention." Typical of Gretchen's attention-getting humor was her way of making fun of her own appearance. She had a long neck and extremely sloping shoulders. Somewhere she found a bed with posts carved to resemble the heads and necks of giraffes. She had herself photographed sitting bolt upright between the posts, looking uncommonly like a third giraffe. The result was an eye-catching Christmas card. With this unconventional turn of mind, Gretchen "had a remarkable ability to find ways to gain access to someone we wanted or needed in the program."

Beginning in March of 1933, when Dorothy was in Switzerland, Gretchen played hostess at a series of teas in Dorothy's New York apartment. Morris showed films and talked about The Seeing Eye, but there was not even a hint of an appeal for support. Gretchen's tea cakes were delectable, and late in the afternoon, tea was followed by mulled wine. The guests were interesting people in their own right. As a result, invitations to Gretchen's select gatherings were envied and sought after.

Thanks to Gretchen's teas, the membership of the sponsoring committee was brought to full strength in May, but it was not unveiled for another six months. On November 14, 1933, the committee held a gala dinner at the Park Lane Hotel. The guest list of nearly 250 included such prominent New York names as Astor, Colgate, Cromwell, Davison, Harriman, Morgan, and Reid. A pleasing innovation was that everyone was personally invited by a hostess and sat at her table. The dinner resembled a collection of private parties, so well planned and executed that there was not an empty chair in the dining room.

To represent its graduates, the school chose not Morris, but Mervyn Sinclair. As a former business executive, and an Ivy League graduate, he was a person with whom this audience would readily identify. Alexander Woollcott, who had his first exposure to The Seeing Eye that night, described Sinclair following Kara through the eddying confusion of the crowd with the stately dignity of a tall ship surrounded by small harbor craft.

To the astonishment of the guests, there was no appeal for funds, but the arousal of Woollcott's interest was worth a fortune. With Dorothy Parker, he drove out to see the school at first hand. The more he learned, the more enthusiastic he became. He vented his enthusiasm in print and on his weekly network broadcast, *The Town Crier*. An appeal for support on one of these broadcasts produced just under $6,000, but the indirect benefits would prove far greater.

In the spring of 1934, The Seeing Eye staged its first benefit, the so-called "Hiss the Villain" party. New York's younger social set, dressed in Gay Nineties' costumes, arrived in horse-drawn carriages, buggies, and one hay wagon for a music-hall performance of an old-fashioned melodrama, *The Drunkard*. The benefit netted The Seeing Eye more than $3,000, and was featured in columns and photographs on the society pages of all the newspapers. But it was never repeated.

Benefits are an expensive and time-consuming way of raising money. They seldom have an educational value, and they therefore produce money for the wrong reasons. The frolicking masqueraders at the "Hiss the Villain" affair learned nothing about The Seeing Eye and would probably have enjoyed themselves equally at a benefit for widows and orphans of the Ku Klux Klan. The same was true of the readers of the society pages. The publicity was irrelevant. As a matter of policy, The Seeing Eye gave up benefits altogether.

The Seeing Eye's fund-raising philosophy evolved into the polar opposite of the "Hiss the Villain" party. Its whole emphasis was on education. If light stands for education, and power for money, then light produced power, instead of the other way round. To a degree this is true of all fund raising, but it was uniquely true of The Seeing Eye. Education was so thoroughly dominant that the term "fund raising" was never used. Moreover, the educational program was not distorted by propaganda, or accompanied by sentimental strains of pity. There was not a hint of B for Bewilderment, L for Loneliness, and the rest. The Seeing Eye had a joyful story to tell. The best way to sell the public was to tell it simply, clearly, without embellishment.

This educational emphasis may have received its initial impetus from a tour of New England private schools by Dorothy Eustis, Morris Frank, and Buddy in the fall of 1932. They went to eleven schools in all, including Phillips Exeter, St. Paul's, and Miss Porter's. The films, Morris, and, most of all, Buddy had an irresistible appeal for school audiences. The student bodies volunteered contributions for Seeing Eye scholarships, and within a few years, Morris and Buddy were covering some 175 private schools from Maine to the Carolinas at regular intervals. Many future business executives or society leaders had their first exposure to The Seeing Eye as members of a school audience.

Meanwhile, the educational program for the adult generations was accelerating. In 1935, the Park Lane dinner was transferred to the Plaza on a much larger scale, with Alexander Woollcott as the chief attraction. The following year, Woollcott's profile of Jack Humphrey in *The New Yorker* conveyed a great deal of information about The Seeing Eye to an influential readership. Woollcott continued to tout the school on his weekly radio program, and there was an ever-increasing number of human-interest stories about Seeing Eye graduates in magazines and newspapers. The photogenic appeal of the dogs was immense.

The Seeing Eye staged gala dinners in Boston and Philadelphia and, with the addition of Marian Jobson to the Strong organization, in Cleveland and Chicago. Jack Humphrey and Alexander Woollcott shared the podium before an audience of 2,600 in Boston's Symphony Hall and nearly 2,000 in Detroit's Orchestra Hall. Booth Tarkington, one of the country's best-loved writers, then recuperating from the temporary blindness of cataracts, addressed an audience in Evanston, Illinois, by long-distance hookup from his home in Indianapolis. In 1935, the school began to publish an informative bulletin, *The Guide*, to spread news of its activities to a growing constituency twice a year.

In the five years since Dorothy had first approached Harold Strong in 1932, his organization had grown enormously, and three of its members, Dickson Hartwell, Marian Jobson, and Margaret Kibbee, felt uncomfortable with its bigness and growing preoccupation with large, impersonal affairs. Dorothy Eustis, too, was unhappy with the direction Harold Strong was taking, and in 1937, when Hartwell, Jobson, and Kibbee formed their own firm, she directed Willi Ebeling to ask for a proposal. Of five public relations firms submitting such proposals, Hartwell, Jobson, and Kibbee was chosen. In consequence, The Seeing Eye's program for public support became far more personal. Significantly, its work was described not as fund raising but as "education and extension."

Extension meant enrollment of annual memberships. These might range anywhere from $5 to $500 and over. There was no attempt to exert pressure for large gifts. A golden egg was no good if it stopped the goose from laying. The school wanted memberships that it could depend on year after year, even if they were modest. Potential donors never felt threatened.

The memberships were enrolled by volunteers. Initially, a sponsoring or executive committee was chosen from among those who had attended the dinners in the various cities. Some were parents of students who had heard Morris Frank at school. Others were prominent members of the Junior League or Council of Jewish Women. With the painstaking organizational work of Marian Jobson, they met in groups of ten, generally in someone's home.

It is significant that the dogs served as a model even here. Dorothy Eustis reasoned that the dogs loved their work and so should the volunteers. And they did. The emphasis of these intimate meetings was primarily educational. Morris attended with Marian Jobson or another staff member, but he was careful both to arrive and to leave alone, thereby demonstrating the freedom of movement a dog made possible. The groups were small so that everyone felt they knew Morris and Buddy personally.

When Morris had left, a staff member organized the

solicitation of memberships. Again the emphasis was educational. If a volunteer protested she did not like to ask for money, she was told not to ask for money, but only to tell the story of The Seeing Eye. The softness of the sell got on the nerves of one flamboyant young socialite from Grosse Point. Entering a meeting, she insisted on whispering because, she said, "The Seeing Eye is so damned well bred!" Requests were almost always to friends or acquaintances. Letters written on personal stationery asking for modest annual memberships for such an appealing cause were hard to resist.

Marian Jobson kept painstakingly accurate lists of the names and addresses of volunteers and those they solicited. There was no duplicate solicitation. Members were asked to give once a year and once a year only. Within a very few years, the school had recruited roughly 1,000 volunteer workers for the committees of various cities. They in their turn enrolled some 15,000, then more than 20,000 memberships. Some were large, $100, $500, or more. The average was about $15, but the volume was more than sufficient to guarantee the school's operating budget. In 1933, the net worth of The Seeing Eye was $43,000. Five years later, it was just under $400,000. In 1943, it surpassed $1 million. By this time, The Seeing Eye was beginning to benefit from a low-key but carefully planned program to encourage testamentary giving that would ultimately bring its assets to more than $25 million.

In strictly material terms, the program of Hartwell, Jobson, and Kibbee was a fund raiser's dream. It reaped a golden harvest. But its educational value was equally successful. Annually, half of The Seeing Eye's 1,000 volunteers were new recruits who were thoroughly grounded in the practice and philosophy of The Seeing Eye and who then sought to communciate what they had learned to thousands of others. Volunteers and members constituted an invaluable information network to carry the school's message across the country. Many of them proved powerful allies in other ways. They helped to open up mass transportation, restaurants, theaters, and other public facilities for guide dogs, to secure jobs for graduates, and to create an awareness of the potentialities of the nation's blind population.

Morris was working on membership enrollment in Chicago one day when a volunteer told him that the head of a cookware factory wanted to see him about a woman employee who was losing her sight. Morris toured the factory and found a job that was suitable for a blind worker. Then he asked the president what had prompted him to turn to The Seeing Eye for advice. He answered that they had been discussing the woman over the family dinner table at Thanksgiving when his son, a student at Deerfield Academy, said he had heard Morris talk about blind factory workers.

In other words The Seeing Eye's unique method of fund raising produced more than financial support. It created understanding. It made the American public aware of a new type of blind people, ready, willing, and able to help themselves, if only they were given the opportunity.

CHAPTER 12

"Never a Dull Moment!"

"NEVER A dull moment at The Seeing Eye!" was the laughing comment that Ibby Hutchinson repeated so often it was ultimately embroidered on a sampler, framed, and hung above her desk at the school. It could have been cast in bronze and mounted over the door the day the first class moved in, because it was true from the beginning. Lila Rich, who became Willi Ebeling's secretary that December, recalls arriving for work to find the heating system had broken down. "There was ice in the goldfish bowl, and Mr. Ebeling was sitting at his desk in his raccoon coat."

Morris Frank and Debby Debetaz were installed in bachelor quarters on the third floor and were soon fast friends. When Debby had completed a class, he would confide the care of the dogs in the kennel to Sita and Adolf, a German couple who served as cook and gardener; then he and Morris headed for New York. At Mandelbaum's, their favorite speakeasy, Buddy sat on a chair between them and was served a saucer of milk with each round of drinks. Once finding Mandelbaum's closed, they were referred to another speakeasy and told to ask for Tony. The name was magical. Every time they asked for Tony, they were brought drinks on the house, but Tony never appeared. They learned later that the sight of Buddy convinced him they were federal agents.

As part of the school's educational program, visitors were frequently invited for meals, and Gretchen Green decided the dining room needed brightening. She cadged a sample roll of wallpaper from Schumacher's in New York, a green ivy-leaf pattern against a cream background, then bought scissors, brushes, paste, and rolls of plain green and cream wallpaper to match. After supper one night, she and Debby papered the entire dining room in cream, then laboriously cut ivy leaves from the green paper and pasted them on the cream background. It took until three in the morning, but they finished the job.

Dorothy Eustis decided that Morris, too, should be spruced up for visitors. She took him to Brooks Brothers and had him outfitted in a sports jacket, gray flannels, and a tattersall vest. Morris was delighted until he discovered he was paying the bill. "It cost me damned near a month's salary, but you didn't argue with the boss!"

In his new finery, Morris was showing a lady visitor through the building when she asked to see "some of the poor dear blind people."

"You're seeing one now," Morris said.

"But your eyes look perfectly normal."

"They should. They cost me twenty-five dollars each."

During the summer of 1933, the gatehouse was remodeled into apartments, one for Dorothy Eustis on the second floor and another for the Humphreys on the first. Nettie Humphrey moved in that fall in time for George to start school, but Jack and Dorothy still spent long periods at Vevey. During the last half of 1933, Debby was there, too, studying guide-dog theory and psychology. In exchange, L'Oeil Qui Voit sent another young Swiss apprentice named Dardel who had a weakness for practical jokes. He delighted in turning on the hot-water taps in the basin, so that the water would run cold on a student taking a shower. He tried this on a student named Messler. It worked the first time, but Messler was a man of considerable size and strength, and the next time, he held Dardel under the water fully clothed until he was soaked to the skin. Dardel never succeeded in adapting to American life and returned to Switzerland in 1934.

In August of that year, a car drove up to the school to deliver a young blind lawyer from Chicago. His name was Herbert Geisler, and he had come down "for the purpose of examining the guide dogs on hand and selecting one which I could take home to Chicago." Amused, Willi Ebeling explained that one did not pick out a guide dog like an animal in a pet shop, and he drove Geisler into Morristown to observe a pair of students in a class under Debetaz.

Undaunted, Geisler said he was prepared to begin training at once and would postpone his return to Chicago as long as necessary. Willi called a hurried conference, and Debby agreed to take on an additional student. In September, Herb Geisler went home with Nubia as his guide.

Chicago had not yet had its first membership enrollment, and nothing had been done to educate the city to the virtues of guide dogs. Banned from public transportation, Geisler and Nubia had to walk miles to and from work; moreover, Nubia was not allowed in Geisler's office building. Geisler had to rent a room for her in a nearby hotel, while he proceeded to his office alone. At lunch time, he came back to feed Nubia and take her out to empty, then returned her to the hotel room for the afternoon. Later, the volunteers of the Chicago committee were there as his allies, but at the outset, he was alone and had to devise his own strategies for breaking down the barriers.

Debby witnessed one such strategy when he stopped to see Geisler on his way home from a class in Berkeley. They met for lunch at the Sherman Hotel, but had hardly been seated in the dining room when the head-waiter objected to Nubia. He refused to hear Geisler's argument that he needed the dog because he was blind. Suddenly, the lawyer handed Nubia's leash to Debby and told him to take her out. When Debby was halfway to the door, Geisler stood up and turned over his table. The headwaiter protested. Geisler answered that he was blind and did not know how to get out of the room without a dog. He turned over a second table and was groping toward a third, when the headwaiter surrendered.

"Sit down quietly now, sir, and you can have your dog."

After lunch, the lawyer treated Debby to a startling tableau. The policeman at a certain street corner had insisted on leading Geisler across the street by the elbow. Even after the lawyer had convinced the policeman not to touch him, he found a way to "help." The moment he saw Geisler approach, he stopped traffic, ran to the corner, squatted down facing Nubia, and gesturing her to follow, backed the entire width of the street in a squatting position. At the curb, he straightened, mopped his brow, and muttered, "Saved his life again."

Thanks to the fighting tactics of graduates like Morris Frank and Herb Geisler, and the educational efforts of Seeing Eye volunteers supported by Alexander Woollcott and Booth Tarkington, the school gradually won acceptance of its dogs in public facilities, but there were some wry by-products of victory. The Delaware and Lackawanna Railroad Station in Morristown bore a sign proclaiming that "the Chicago Express will stop to discharge Seeing Eye passengers and corpses only."

Before Morristown had developed civic pride as the home of The Seeing Eye, there were problems with the local citizens. The school was using public space as its classroom, and this inevitably entailed some inconvenience for the residents. When a dog came too close to a moving car in the street, the instructor slapped the fender with a *"Pfui!"* The sound of a thud on a rear fender was a chilling experience for nervous drivers. Small children carried ice cream cones and candy bars at a height just level with a dog's nose and mouth, and occasionally they vanished as if by magic as a German shepherd shot past. One elderly woman stepped back suddenly into the path of an oncoming student and broke her hip. Others were bumped or had their feet stepped on by students who were awkward in following their dogs.

The bank had the only revolving door in town, and the school received permission to expose its dogs to this type of obstacle. One day an instructor was just halfway through the door when his dog suffered an attack of diarrhea. His desperate attempts to clean up the mess were complicated by a continuous flow of customers entering the bank.

Dog lovers complained of cruelty, but even kindly intervention could be disconcerting. In the early years, students were trained with white canes. When Debby found that one of his students was confused by the cane, he relieved him of it and sent him off on a solo. As he was looking after the student, an old lady offered to lead him across the street. He accepted, thanked her, and was observing his student on the other side, when another woman offered to take him back across.

In February 1934, Dorothy Eustis closed L'Oeil Qui Voit, and in December, Jack undertook to train a class of eight American apprentices. This increased activity on the streets of Morristown and compounded the public relations problem. Fortunately, the Messler who had drenched Dardel was a local resident with relatives on the police force, and Jack Humphrey cultivated the friendship of the chief.

This was helpful, because one of Jack's training techniques was alarming to onlookers. Periodically, he drove down a street where students or apprentices were working their dogs and wheeled suddenly into driveways in their path to give traffic checks. It was a questionable training technique, because, after one experience, dogs learned to identify the sound of Jack's engine and were ready for him, but Jack seemed to enjoy it for its own sake. Once when he had executed two or three spectacular cuts on Maple Street, a State Motor Vehicle inspector who was passing through confiscated his license for reckless endangerment. To the secret delight of his apprentices, Jack had to walk to the police station to square accounts with the chief.

Visitors to the school became a problem. If they followed students too closely on the streets, they distracted the dogs. Some were numbingly tactless. One woman spent lunch making invidious comparisons of dogs in a voice of brass. "Your dog isn't half as handsome as Mrs. Jones's," or "The dog with the man from Pittsburgh looks kind of sickly." Eventually, visitors were strictly limited, but occasionally they came unasked.

Ibby Hutchinson recalls a Hindu woman complete with sari and caste mark who appeared without warning late one afternoon to announce she was an official representative of work for the blind in New Delhi. At her haughty insistence, she was put up at a Morristown hotel at Seeing Eye expense and spent the following morning at the school insulting one member of the staff after another. Following lunch, she cached all the leftover cold cuts and rolls she could gather into a basket she carried and boarded the New York bus threatening to report The Seeing Eye's inhospitality to her government. Inquiry revealed that she had no official status whatever and was simply an impostor.

The school did not need visitors to inject variety into its classes. The students came from widely divergent backgrounds, regions, educational levels, and walks of life. At various times, they included a woman water colorist who was still painting and exhibiting, a black pugilist who had once fought champion Tony Zale, a former major-league baseball player from the Chicago White Sox, an Eskimo, and a Russian nobleman who claimed to have been blinded by God as punishment for having killed so many men. In a single class, I once had with me an ex-gambler, a veteran who had lost his left hand as well as his eyes, a black cabinetmaker, a hypnotist, and the first blind, pregnant student to attend the Sorbonne on a Fulbright scholarship. Hector Chevigny, author of definitive works on the Russian settlement of North America, also wrote a popular radio serial, *The Second Mrs. Burton*. Bernice Clifton and her dog were much in demand on the lecture circuit. Roy de Groot, gourmet author of *A Feast for All Seasons,* appeared regularly on NBC's *Today Show*. Katharine Smith was a columnist for the *Buffalo Express*.

Exposing this variegated human mixture to an experience not unlike boot camp produced some novel situations. Occasionally, there were flare-ups. Under the strain of the course, students came to words and at least twice, even to blows. Jack Humphrey got into a feud with an impertinent male student who insisted on smoking a pipe while working his dog. One evening when the class was on its way to give the dogs an airing, Jack spied the offending pipe from his living room window. Throwing it open, he shouted at the student, who removed his pipe, turned it upside down to prove it was empty, and insolently replaced it in his mouth. But the tale of the smart alec smoker has an Aesopian ending. As a news vendor in the Bronx, he defied Seeing Eye rules by leaving his dog behind to guard the newsstand, while he went to lunch by himself in a nearby diner. He was not using his dog when he fell into an open manhole and was killed.

There are many stories about the early days: about the time Arthur Meeker, the burly groundskeeper, collared a suspicious character snooping in the lilacs who turned out to be Henry Colgate, chairman of the board, inspecting the bushes he had donated to the school; about the time the cooks quit without notice and Aunt Mary Campbell and Ibby Hutchinson were pressed into service to cook salmon caught personally by Mr. Colgate; about the time Mervyn Sinclair's Kara lay on Willi Ebeling's spanking new Panama hat and Aunt Mary spent two hours trying to reblock it with her hand iron; and about the time Agnes Fowler, a board member, donned blue jeans to muck out the kennels and was asked for a date by the Polish kennel man.

Nor are all the stories about the early days. In the 1960s after Dorothy, Jack, Willi, and Morris were out of the picture, George Werntz, Willi Ebeling's successor, had an idea for a public relations photograph. One of the ken nel men allowed his beard to grow for three days. He was then outfitted with old clothes, dark glasses, a tin cup, and a sign, "BLIND," and paired with a scrawny mongrel at the end of a huge rusty chain. The photograph was to lampoon the obsolete stereotype of the blind beggar, but while George Werntz and the photographer were still in the act of posing their subjects on the streets of Morristown, a gentleman in a homburg paused, put a hand in the pocket of his tailor-made suit, and dropped fifty cents into the tin cup. For all the school's educational efforts, old stereotypes died hard.

CHAPTER 13

The Challenge
of Freedom

"I was out of my cage the first day I walked down the street with my dog," a graduate exulted. "I was free, and that was the way I was going to stay." An Allentown worker who picked up three graduates with their dogs to drive them home from the school observed, "It is as if they had been released from prison, having been sentenced for life."

Prison is often used as a metaphor for blindness, and its psychological impact is often very similar. One type of convict becomes mutinous, bitterly resentful of everything and everybody, and there is a similar type among those who go blind. They become rebellious, resistant to any suggestion from outside, but among both prisoners and blind people, they are in the minority.

In order to survive in an environment in which he is not free to make decisions, the average convict retreats into himself. Consciously or not, he cultivates the passivity and resignation that enable him to endure the loss of freedom. The model prisoner has become so accustomed to responding automatically to external stimuli that when he is released, he is nearly incapable of making the simplest decisions. As a Trenton State Prison inmate put it, "When he goes through a door, he doesn't know whether to turn left or right. When he goes into a restaurant, he doesn't know how to choose a meal. When he goes to sleep, he doesn't know how to wake up."

Blindness can have the same paralyzing effect on the will and the decision-making faculty. Many blind people passively accept the estimate of their helplessness thrust on them by their family, friends, or agency. They become model workers resigned to a life of making brooms or caning chairs.

Students bring attitudes varying from resignation to rebelliousness to The Seeing Eye, but it is virtually impossible to graduate with them. They begin to change even before their arrival.

The decision to get a dog reflects the determination to change the dependency on family or friends. The young sons of a Carolina farmer were so fearful that their blind father would hurt himself that they insisted on guiding him around the farm on his daily chores. To the question of why he wanted a dog, he answered simply, "So my sons can go to school, and I can go where I like." Booth Tarkington described a girl whose family "won't let her have a dog, because they think a guide dog will make them conspicuous, put them in the wrong, look as if they wouldn't take the trouble to lead the poor thing around themselves." This girl was a prisoner of her family's tyrannical charity. Her declaration of independence would have begun with her departure for The Seeing Eye.

A young wife who wanted a dog but whose "husband said no" touched on the most humiliating aspect of blindness. "My experience has been that people kill me with kindness. As long as I act feebleminded and partially paralyzed, I get along fine. I feel there is nothing wrong with my mind since losing my sight. I feel just as capable of making certain decisions as I ever did." During the blindness of his cataract operations, Booth Tarkington had a glimpse of the same humiliation when a friend read aloud from a book the words, "He felt himself as unlike his fellow beings, as if he had been blind or an idiot." Tarkington commented, "Among the nuisances of blindness to which I was imaginatively looking forward had not been that of relegation to the status of an idiot."

Many students coming to The Seeing Eye were surprised that the staff addressed them all as Mr., Mrs., or Miss. They had so long been treated as children, they were accustomed to being called by their first names only. Each Mr., Mrs., and Miss was a reminder that they were adults.

The shock of this courtesy was followed fast by the shock of the daily schedule at Morristown. They were waked at half-past five in the morning to dress and take their dogs out to empty in "the Park," a large rectangle of gravel behind the house. The trip to the Park was a formidable challenge in itself. It began at the top of the steps on the second floor and proceeded as follows: Down five steps, turn right on landing, find top step, down five steps, turn right on landing, find top step, down ten steps to hall, cross hall, find knob of inner door, drop harness, open door, go through door and close door, pick up harness, find knob to outer door, drop harness, open, go through and close outer door, pick up harness, cross porch, find top step, down porch steps, turn right on sidewalk for twenty paces past corner of building, turn right and walk forward to edge of driveway, pause, cross driveway to opposite edge, pause, forward on walk about fifteen paces to next driveway, pause, cross driveway, pause, forward into Park.

In the course of this trip, there were at least eighteen commands to be given in the proper order with the proper inflection and accompanying body movements. Each command properly obeyed must be rewarded by a cheerful "Atta good girl!" Students must avoid crowding each other. Each student must open and close the inner and outer door unaided to get practice. The dogs must be corrected for sniffing or being distracted by other dogs. After the right turn at the foot of the porch steps, there was a stone balustrade that could inflict a painful charley horse in the thigh of the unwary. There were no curbs on the driveway, so it was easy for dogs to run the edges and difficult for novices to detect that they had. Instructors posted along the route pointed out errors.

Once in the Park, the students removed their dogs' harnesses and followed them around a large gravel rectangle on long leash, being careful not to get dogs and leashes tangled. Emptying on leash was something the dogs had not been taught, and it took time to learn. With two classes in session, there were sixteen human minds focusing solely on canine bowels and bladders. This was faintly amusing, but the amusement wore thin as a quarter of an hour in the chill dawn stretched to twenty or thirty minutes. When the dogs had emptied at last, the route had to be walked in reverse to the second floor to wait for breakfast at seven o'clock.

The first trip started at eight. Four humans and four dogs climbed into a station wagon one at a time, and the instructor drove them to Morristown. There were six or seven routes, varying from a few blocks on Maple Street to the four-mile "boy scout route." The dogs walked at a rate of three and a half miles an hour. After 1931, a rigid U-shaped harness handle replaced the flexible strap Morris had used with Buddy and gave a more precise definition of the dog's direction. The dogs were bigger, stronger, and harder than the dogs the school now uses. It was not unusual for a student to drop out from inability to stand the strain, but many of them returned later after hardening themselves with exercise at home.

Mrs. Rita Duren described the impact of her turnover with a dog given the appropriate name of Urge. "My experience of The Seeing Eye was explosive. It dynamited me out of a protective shroud I had built around myself. I was bewildered, and cogs of my brain didn't work, but there was no going back. Urge was always pulling forward, and the staff was there to say in effect, 'What is making you hesitate? The world is yours!' "

Mrs. Duren had been blind and relatively immobile for many years. "I was tense with the abrupt transition from slow motion to speed and danger. I was dying from being jerked around by the dog, not having enough hands for dog, comb and brush, and feed pan, from trying to remember routes, from managing the stairs and trying to keep my body intact."

There were many individual problems. Mr. Finch had trained his own dogs for eleven years. They had guided him on leash, and the changeover to a rigid harness handle was not easy. "I had eleven years of acquired bad habits to unlearn in three weeks." Emil Buchko was only about four feet tall, crippled, and unable to ascend a curb without the helping pull of his dog, which had to be specially trained for him. Many students had only the most rudimentary notions of orientation. Others had difficulty in giving commands with authority. Mr. Whitman, who was partially deaf, remained stalled so long at one corner giving quavering "forwards" to Betts, that he finally lost his temper completely and shouted, "Betts, forward! Right! Left! Take your pick, dammit, but do something!!!"

Incidents of this sort seemed hilariously funny, and if there were anxieties, confusion, and physical discomfort to overcome, they were outweighed by an inordinate amount of laughter. I myself went to my first class at The Seeing Eye with some of the same dread I would have entertained at the prospect of three weeks' retreat in a Trappist monastery. To my surprise, I laughed more and had more fun than I had as a member of the Princeton Triangle Club touring its musical comedy to a dozen cities from New York to St. Louis with parties every night. What was so funny? Nothing. Except that I had come with a heavy heart, and suddenly my heart was high. I have witnessed the same thing in dozens of others.

Part of it is the exhilaration of that first walk. Stepping out with the breathtaking new freedom of the tugging harness handle, students feel their backs and shoulders straighten. They feel suddenly taller, like men and women again. They praise their dogs with laughing voices and become laughing men and women. "The habit of bestowing praise is a very beneficial one for human beings to acquire," wrote Booth Tarkington. "It is likely to enlarge their hearts." At The Seeing Eye, students who must bestow praise on their dogs literally hundreds of times a day feel their hearts enlarging.

Dogs offer students another kind of freedom they rarely receive from human guides. As one woman put it, "A dog would not be guilty of imposing her wishes on me because she felt that I was blind and was incapable of thinking. She would not enrage me to tears by insisting that she spread my biscuit or butter my toast. She would not insist on taking my arms and half-carrying me down steps with the result that I never quite know just where my foot is going to land. She would not do that, because she would 'feel safer,' regardless of how safe or unsafe I feel."

In other words, guide dogs do not impose their wills on their masters, and they do not condescend to them. They look up to them, and the sense of being looked up to is one some students may not have had for a long time.

The impact of the affection between a dog and master is transforming. One young man who came to the school in a state of active rebellion against practically everything gradually mellowed. He had arrived unkempt and carelessly dressed, but he began to take pains with his appearance, combing his hair before every meal, shaving daily instead of every two or three days, and even borrowing his roommate's brush and polish to shine his shoes. When asked what had come over him he answered, "Well, you know, my dog is such a lady." The head of a local welfare board gave his impression of a young father just returned from The Seeing Eye: "I have never known anyone changed so much in four weeks as Mr. Z. He now holds his head up, throws his shoulders back, is in better physical condition, and for the first time since loss of sight is anxious to work and support his family."

Changes of this sort were not due solely to dogs, for the school was teaching more than guide-dog technique. Ibby Hutchinson read students their mail in private, and the readings led easily into conversation. Once they had their dogs, she said, they would be spending far more time in the sighted world, getting out into public places, doing things they had not done for years, if ever. They might like some suggestions other students had found helpful. She gave them tips on grooming and taking care of their nails. One of the most sensitive subjects to broach was the appearance of their eyes. I can illustrate from personal experience. I had been blind about four months when I had a visit from a college roommate.

"Putnam," he told me, "you ought to be wearing dark glasses."

Inwardly I winced. The bullet that had severed my optic nerves had not touched my eyes, and although fluids collecting behind my eyeballs had created considerable swelling, that had nearly subsided, and I assumed that except for my closed eyelids, I looked quite normal. None of my large family had hinted anything to the contrary. It took the candor of a peer to inform me that my lids were red and one eye was distractingly part way open. He did not persuade me immediately. It took some convincing, but he stuck to it, and I have blessed him many times since.

Many blind people are harder to convince. Those who have been born blind can have no idea how important the appearance of eyes can be. Their attitude is, "If I can put up with my blindness, so can you." Frequently, their families support them against what they regard as an unfeeling attack. Some blind people seem to feel that wearing dark glasses will draw attention to their blindness, unaware that many sighted people wear dark glasses, and that their eyes are far more distracting than glasses.

A few blind people seem to feel they are entitled to ignore social conventions by virtue of their blindness, but The Seeing Eye's position is that if you want to be treated as an equal in the sighted world, you must conform to the standards of the sighted world, including its visual standards. If you do not wish to be treated as a blind person, you should not draw attention to your blindness, visually or in other ways. Ibby Hutchinson was so completely and manifestly a lady that almost no one could take offense at her suggestions, and she set students of both sexes straight on many details of dress, manners, and appearance.

The total impact of the school amazed observers. A social worker wrote of one graduate, "I have never seen such a change in anybody in four weeks. He has developed character, initiative, and independence. He is neat and clean and so polite now, and so much more particular about his person. I do not see how you do it in such a short period of training."

Years later, Albert Gayzagian recalled the importance of some advice Willi Ebeling had given him on his eighteenth birthday. "I had come to your office to discuss my leaving for home. When I rose to leave, I failed to start in the right direction. I was not going straight for the door. You advised me to always pay careful attention how I entered an office, so that I could make a good exit and not give the person I had been talking to the impression that I was not capable of getting about." This little tip, he said, had been important in his success with the John Hancock Insurance Company.

Victor Pares Collazo wrote, "I will always remember that, when I reached the school, my whole personality was disturbed, that I was afraid to face my new life, and that you all contributed to help me in my moral and psychological reconstruction. I do not doubt that, if I am writing from this desk [as a district judge in Puerto Rico] it is greatly due to the hearty push you gave me."

The "moral and psychological reconstruction" of a

big Pennsylvania Dutchman named Pfeiffer surprised even The Seeing Eye. His wife was opposed to his getting a dog. She said he could get around the block with a cane, but Pfeiffer replied, "Yes, and the block is my prison." He enrolled in the school, and because he came from a sleepy village, Debetaz decided he would make a likely partner for Lisa.

Lisa was an excellent guide in every respect but one. In training, she and Debetaz had been at the corner of Park Place and South Street when a freight elevator emerged clattering through the sidewalk. It made such an indelible impression on Lisa that he was never again able to get her to pass that corner. Nothing could persuade her, and because guide dogs must be educated, not trained, she had to be persuaded, not forced. However, since Pfeiffer's little village had no freight elevators, he decided that Lisa would do for him nicely.

The turnover was successful, but about three months later, Debetaz saw Pfeiffer and Lisa get off the bus and walk up the driveway. Sure something had gone wrong, he hurried to meet them. Pfeiffer was all smiles. He had been off on a little excursion to Harrisburg, Philadelphia, and New York. He was just stopping by to say hello. In response to Debby's questions, he said that Lisa had guided him through all the noise and confusion that New York could offer. Half disbelieving, Debby asked whether he would mind going down to Morristown so he could watch them work. Pfeiffer agreed, and following them around the streets, Debby directed them to the fateful corner of Park Place and South. Unhesitatingly, Lisa guided her master past the very spot where the elevator had popped up, then looked over her shoulder at him. Her look, he says, spoke clearly: "I'll do it for this guy, but not for you."

The block had been Pfeiffer's prison. When Debby turned him over with Lisa, he had thought she would give him the freedom of his village, but the love and gratitude he had lavished on Lisa had unlocked the door to a much wider world. There were no prisons now.

CHAPTER 14

The Achilles' Heel

WITH HER customary clarity of perception, Dorothy Eustis labeled the difficulty of finding suitable instructors as the Achilles' heel of The Seeing Eye. The problem had arisen first in the summer of 1928, when she and Jack had begun to look for an instructor for Morris Frank. Since Germany had been turning out guide dogs for twelve years, they had assumed there would be a plentiful supply of competent instructors available. They discovered that, while there were many apprentices capable of teaching certain aspects of the work under supervision, there were only a handful sufficiently familiar with all phases to provide such supervision.

The experience at L'Oeil Qui Voit confirmed the difficulty of the problem. Of more than fifty apprentices who enrolled, only three qualified as full instructors. Liakhoff, a Russian, went to England to carry on the work begun there by Humphrey and Debetaz. Gabriel became chief instructor in Italy. Only Debetaz was left for the American Seeing Eye.

In February 1934, Dorothy Eustis closed down L'Oeil Qui Voit, and in June, Jack Humphrey set forth the plan of an American school for instructors. In effect, it was an Americanization of L'Oeil Qui Voit. The Swiss school had been educating instructors, and the instructors in turn had

165

been educating guide dogs supplied by Fortunate Fields. Many of these had been sold to The Seeing Eye and sent to the United States for classes with blind students.

The new American school would perform a similar function. Jack Humphrey, his salary still paid by Fortunate Fields, would be its head. Since most of the expenses would be underwritten by a fund donated by Helen Hubbard, the woman who had financed Jack Humprhey's scholarly publications, it would be called the Hubbard School for Instructors. The dogs that the apprentices educated would be sold to The Seeing Eye for classes with American students. Physically, of course, everything was located on the Whippany property, and the Hubbard apprentices taught Seeing Eye students under the supervision of Humhprey and Debetaz. Only male apprentices would be accepted. Adelaide Clifford and Missy Doudge had done excellent work, but Adelaide had not been able to take the mental and physical strain, and Missy had fallen into the most dangerous of traps for professional women, marriage. Women, it was decided, were a poor risk.

Jack planned a comprehensive curriculum for the Hubbard apprentices. Their course would last four years and be "the equivalent of a college education." In addition to the theory and practice of guide-dog education, they would study and hear lectures on such topics as animal psychology, animal physiology, animal husbandry, principles of breeding, genetics, and the physiology of the eye. When Jack typed them up, the Hubbard lectures filled 3,000 pages.

The school opened in December 1934. Eight apprentices were selected from approximately a hundred applicants. They lived on the grounds of The Seeing Eye in a remodeled barn and began by going through the entire routine of a class just as if they were students, wearing blindfolds from the time they woke up until they went to bed at night. The hours were long, the work was hard, and the pay was low, but the country was in the depths of the Depression, and a job of any sort was prized.

Dorothy's feelings about instructors' salaries was revealed in an interview with Debetaz at the close of his first year in America. Noting he had been paid seventy-five dollars a month above his room and board, she asked how much he had put aside. He had to admit he had saved nothing. She expressed the fear he was squandering his pay on beer and frivolous amusements. She advised him to open a savings account at once. Meanwhile, she had a gift for him. If he expected a cash bonus as a nest egg for his savings account he was disappointed. It was a signed photograph of herself.

The management of The Seeing Eye regarded apprentices as subordinates who were expected to keep their place. When two apprentices approached Dorothy Eustis for a raise on the morning a class of students was to begin, she sensed blackmail and did not hesitate. Tapping on the glass of her office for the bookkeeper, she had her draw checks for two weeks salary and told the young men to have their personal effects off the premises by nightfall. "She would have fired the whole staff the same way," Morris insists. "Nobody threatened the boss and got away with it."

Willi Ebeling was reasonable and courteous, but subordinates who argued or complained found themselves backed up against the mantel of his office. Jack Humphrey was just, but he expected hard work, and he minced no words.

Ned Myrose applied for a job as apprentice in the fall of 1937. Jack told him he would have to spend the first six months working in the kennels and offered him fifty dollars a month plus board and lodging. Myrose took it. He remembers Jack as a harder worker than any subordinate. Many a morning, he was in his office two hours before daylight typing up the Hubbard lectures, and he was all over the school and the streets of Morristown the rest of the day.

"I used to love to hear him talk," Myrose says, "but he could be a terror."

Once when an apprentice was having difficulty teaching a stubborn dog obedience, Jack stepped in to demonstrate. But the dog continued mulish. For once, Jack lost his temper with an animal. Fetching it a clout on the ear, he spun on the apprentice, pointed his finger, and snapped, "If I ever catch you doing that, I'll fire you on the spot."

Another time, he gave one of Myrose's women students a traffic check and ran over her foot. She had habitually taken another step after her dog had stopped, and Jack decided this was the only way to teach her.

He coddled apprentices no more than students. When Curtiss Weeman was taking a blindfold test, Jack allowed his dog to walk him into a steel post at full speed. Weeman split his forehead, but Jack's position was that, since apprentices were asking their blind students to trust their dogs, they should learn from experience what could happen when a dog was not trustworthy.

Debby recalls a blindfold test in England. He had worked one dog before breakfast. When Jack showed up unexpectedly over coffee and suggested a blindfold test, Debby figured to have an easy time of it by walking the same dog over the same route. In the middle of the fourth block, the dog stopped in an area where Debby knew there was no obstruction. When she refused to budge after repeated *forwards* Debby committed the unpardonable sin. He stepped in front of his dog and into a scaffolding that had been erected during his breakfast. "Jack was across the street laughing, and I was pulling splinters from my forehead the rest of the morning."

Of the first eight Hubbard apprentices, only Weeman and Hauptmann became instructors. In the fall of 1938, Jack started a new class, this time recruited from the ranks of college graduates. Of 150 applicants, the school took six. Only three became instructors. They were Harold Dickerman, Robert Lee, and Richard Northrup.

The life of a guide-dog instructor had certain com-
pensations. For the right sort of man, exercise in the open
air was preferable to sitting behind a desk. Working ten to
twelve hard-pulling dogs ten to fifteen miles a day kept
apprentices lean and muscular, but some broke under the
physical strain. Others developed problems with their backs.

Dogfights were a hazard. As the demand for dogs grew,
the school had to abandon its policy of using bitches ex-
clusively. Until 1939, these bitches were not spayed, and
their coming into season stimulated aggression among the
males. There were some bloody battles in the kennels. Once,
wading into a snarling pack, Northrup was struck in the
chest by a big boxer and went down. Dickerman later
claimed that his intervention at that moment may have
saved Northrup's life.

Myrose had one class with four males that hated each
other and four bitches of which two were in season. "Maybe
you think that wasn't a scramble, keeping them apart in the
recreation room!"

The safety of eight pairs of dogs and students was a
heavy responsibility. After the first couple of days, student-
dog pairs worked two at a time, one in front of the other.
The lead pair waited at down curbs for the other to come
up, so that they would not get too far separated. To keep
both pairs in view, the instructor posted himself in the
rear and had to move fast if the lead student ran into
trouble. He first had to order the rear student to put his
dog at sit, so that he could give the lead student his undivided attention. Once, failing to take this precaution, Ned
Myrose found himself racing forward after one student
while looking over his shoulder at the other. A moment
later, he was doing a somersault over a fire hydrant.

The nervous strain was immense. As experienced graduates returning for second dogs appeared in numbers, the
problem eased. Graduates were able to reassure first timers
on the capabilities of guide dogs, and they required less
strict supervision, but even veterans could make stupid

mistakes. During a class for my second dog, Wick, I commanded him forward at a busy intersection. I was unaware of a large puddle in the gutter in front of us. To avoid it, Wick gave a bound, pulling both leash and harness out of my hand. It was an inexcusable lapse on my part, and Dickerman's heart must have been in his mouth as he leapt into the traffic to retrieve Wick. At any given moment, instructors must be prepared to rescue students from unexpected cars, ditches, overhangs, and their own mistakes. Hauptmann broke under the nervous strain and had to retire a little more than a year after his graduation.

Instructors developed strong bonds of affection for their dogs during the three months before class. The dogs loved to work, and when the door of the truck in which they were driven to Morristown was opened, they greeted their heroes with furiously wagging tails and clamored to be the first. This was heartwarming, but once instructors had paired their dogs with their new masters, they had to ignore those pleading eyes and wagging tails, so that the dogs would transfer their affection to their masters.

It was a thrill to watch a novice taking his first walk, but it was painful to observe the bafflement of a dog whose master had given the wrong command or failed to follow a clear signal and clumsily stepped on its paw. Puzzled by its new master's ineptitude, a dog would look to the instructor to ask, "Why are you doing this to me?"

Some of the students could be exasperating. Directed left, they turned right. They got lost on the way to the dining room, were late for the trip into town, and discovered only after they were halfway there that they had forgotten their gloves or their dog's muzzle. It was difficult to be patient with a slow-witted student who was spoiling a favorite dog.

During the three months' preparation, apprentices worked twelve hours a day, six days a week. During class they slept within earshot of the students in the main house and were on call twenty-four hours a day, seven days a week.

The last student in a class generally left on a Friday. This gave the lucky apprentice an entire weekend free before starting to train a new string of dogs the following Monday. It is not surprising that so few of those who enrolled lasted the full four years. One recruit had second thoughts during his first night and left the following morning.

Despite the difficulty of training instructors, The Seeing Eye had been graduating a larger number of students each year. From a low of eleven in 1931, the number rose to forty in 1934 and surpassed one hundred for the first time in 1938. There were not enough rooms in the main house to accommodate all the students. A temporary solution was to start a class in the main house, then after two weeks to move the men students into the old apprentice quarters to make room for a new class. The construction of a wing that included a new kitchen and dining room downstairs and six bedrooms and a recreation room upstairs enabled two classes to run simultaneously. It was opened in January 1940, and The Seeing Eye graduated a record 144 students that year.

Finding suitable dogs for so many students was another problem. To avoid any semblance of conflict of interest, Willi Ebeling had given up his breeding program when he joined the staff in 1932. Fortunate Fields continued to supply dogs for some years, but Dorothy Eustis closed it down in 1938. The school sought out dogs from breeders known to Dorothy, Willi, or Jack. Shepherds were in the majority, but Jack felt that the qualities making for a good guide were more a function of the individual than of the breed, and the school was soon training boxers, Labradors, Dobermans, Briards, golden retrievers, and mixed breeds. Ultimately, more than thirty breeds were represented, but good dogs of any breed were hard to come by.

A number of dogs were donated by owners who could not keep them for some reason, but they sometimes changed their minds. Two elderly sisters from nearby Bernardsville offered a beautiful shepherd male because one of them was allergic to dog hair. Three days later they telephoned tearfully to ask to have him back. When the allergy was aggravated, they donated him again. In all, the dog went back and forth from Bernardsville to Morristown eight times before the ninth donation proved final.

Dogs of this sort accustomed to a home environment did not adapt well to kennel life. Clean and friendly in a family setting, they became filthy and snappish in confinement. Often they rolled in their own excrement. It seemed impossible that such foul-smelling and ill-tempered animals could ever make proper companions for a blind graduate, but as soon as they were taken into the main house during class, they became their old selves, perfectly housebroken and amiable.

Another source of supply was a Mr. Krause, who came by two or three times a month with a truckload of dogs he had picked up all over the county. "Probably stole some of them," Myrose supposes. It is amusing to think of the aristocratic Dorothy Eustis as president of an organization that trafficked in stolen dogs, but the need was great, and the dogs Jack Humphrey picked from Krause's assortment were sound, healthy, and intelligent.

In 1940, The Seeing Eye began breeding its own shepherds. Unhappily, none of the Fortunate Fields breeding stock had been preserved, and the war in Europe put dogs from Germany out of reach. Jack Humphrey collected seed stock from a variety of sources. They were housed in a new kennel built on the Whippany property. When nine of the twenty-one brood bitches proved unsuitable as mothers, they were spayed and trained as guides.

The breeding program was barely under way when the United States was drawn into the war. Partly to relieve the problem of care during the manpower shortage and partly to isolate the puppies from the danger of contagion in the kennels, Jack hit on an ingenious idea. At Fortunate Fields, pups had been farmed out to peasant families to gain the social experience that is so valuable for working dogs. Jack persuaded the 4-H Club of Morris County to make the rearing of Seeing Eye puppies one of their regular programs. The Seeing Eye agreed to pay food costs of about five dollars a month for each dog, and thirty-five puppies were farmed out in 1942. From this modest beginning would grow one of The Seeing Eye's major programs and one later adopted by other guide-dog schools.

World War II affected The Seeing Eye in a number of important ways. Debetaz, Weeman, Myrose, Dickerman, Lee, and Northrup were given draft deferments, but the kennel men who also taught obedience were lost to the armed forces. The kennel maids, who replaced the men, were incapable of teaching the dogs obedience, and that had to be added to the work load of the instructors. The war made it impossible to recruit new apprentices, and worst of all, it took Jack Humphrey. In June 1942, he entered the Coast Guard with the rank of lieutenant commander to organize and run a school for dog trainers for the armed forces.

Jack had worked hard and brilliantly for The Seeing Eye, but it never occupied his entire horizon to the extent it did for Willi or Morris. Until 1938, he was on the pay-roll of Fortunate Fields, which he still visited regularly, and was technically only on loan to The Seeing Eye. So distinguished a scientist as Alexis Carrel regarded The Seeing Eye as a frivolous interruption of Jack's real work. At Fortunate Fields, his scientific methods had raised the percentage of dogs trained and put into service relative to the number bred from 16 to 94 percent, but there were infinite areas of genetic research with dogs to be explored. When Dorothy closed Fortunate Fields, he was shattered. Willi Ebeling recalled, "I never saw a sadder man than Jack when Mrs. Eustis stopped breeding the shepherd. Tears rolled out of Jack's eyes. He felt he had only begun."

Wholly confined to The Seeing Eye, he occupied his restless mind by constant experimentation with newer methods. He was never content. In the year the school graduated more than 100 dogs for the first time, he devised and put down on paper a scheme of instruction calculated to turn out four times that number. His decision to go into the service may have reflected his restless craving for further challenge. In the course of the war, he grew away from The Seeing Eye, and by the time he left the service, his old friend and former employer, Dorothy Eustis, was dying. As Willi put it, "Jack went back to his first love, the West" and settled in Arizona.

Meanwhile, the war had been exerting pressures on the school. The day after the United States declared war, the board of trustees resolved to provide all qualified blind veterans with dogs free of charge either to themselves or to the government and to offer them preferment on the waiting list. At Seeing Eye expense, Morris Frank undertook travels that kept him on the road for months at a time to visit army, navy, and veterans' hospitals. There he showed films and lectured to doctors, nurses, and staffs on the treatment and rehabilitation of blind people. He distributed copies of a booklet prepared by The Seeing Eye under the direction of Mary Campbell, *The Newly Blind*. It embodied the school's distinctive philosophy of rehabilitation and was probably the most influential piece of literature The Seeing Eye ever produced. Morris and Buddy visited a total of ninety-six hospitals, and in addition to his other efforts, Morris conducted extensive interviews with blind veterans. Many of these later came to the school, and by 1950, The Seeing Eye had provided dogs for 163 veterans. War industry was another cause for a sharp increase in the demand for dogs. It was starved for manpower, and employers were willing to hire handicapped workers as never before. Blind men and women needed dogs to get to their jobs, and by the end of the war, approximately 15 percent of the school's thousand-odd graduates were working in war industries.

The war stimulated a boom in guide-dog schools. In

the thirties, Sinykin, Weber, another German named Kreimer, and several others had trained guide dogs for blind people, but the number was insignificant. In 1939, Leader Dogs for the Blind was established in Michigan, but it began modestly. Now a law promising federal funds for guide dogs for blind veterans produced a rash of new "schools." By 1942, there were twenty-seven, nineteen of them in California alone. Most of these were one- or two-man operations, and when the California legislature required licensing based on blindfold tests for all trainers in traffic, fifteen of these "schools" evaporated. Others were hand-to-mouth operations, but Leader Dogs grew, and so did the newly established Guide Dogs for the Blind, first in Los Gatos and later at San Rafael, California.

Willi Ebeling did not have a high opinion of the competition. Some seemed more interested in raising money than training dogs. None approached Seeing Eye standards of safety, and none required a small financial obligation on the part of the students. Donaldson, who headed Guide Dogs for the Blind, had failed as a Hubbard apprentice in Jack's first class, as had his successor, William Johns. Willi Ebeling's chief fear was that the slipshod work of one of these schools might result in an accident that would reflect discredit on the guide-dog movement as a whole. It seems not to have occurred to him that rival schools might one day pose a threat to his own staff.

A more immediate threat was the booming postwar economy. Security was no longer the recompense for long hours and low wages it had been during the Depression. In 1945, Northrup left the school to go into business. Several promising new apprentices were enrolled and the situation appeared to have stabilized, but trouble was brewing under the surface. Agnes Fowler, a trustee who had voluntarily worked in the kennels throughout the war, felt a bond of sympathy with the instructors. She urged Willi Ebeling to improve salaries substantially, but he refused. It was his duty to be thrifty with philanthropic dollars, and he could point out that Debetaz had worked a lot harder for less pay and under more difficult conditions.

Any comparison of the instructors with either Humphrey or Debetaz was both unfavorable and unfair. Jack was a genius with animals. At L'Oeil Qui Voit, he finished a dog in only twelve days' time and scored 62 on the blindfold test, just two points short of perfect. Debby had trained dogs and classes in Pittsburgh, Berkeley, San Francisco, Harrisburg, Washington, Denver, and Los Angeles under conditions no instructor had to put up with in Morristown. In Kansas City, he was attacked on the street by a hysterical woman with two policemen, claiming the dog he was training was her Fritz. Happily, the dog was a bitch and no Fritz, as he could prove by lifting her forepaws. In the White Curtain Hotel in Berkeley, a dog medicated for worms had failed to respond for 36 hours, then emptied in the hotel dining room at luncheon with 160 guests at table. Debby hustled his blind students into their rooms and fled for the afternoon to give the management time to cool off before even attempting an apology. No apology would have been necessary in the dining room at Whippany.

Debby's capacity for work bordered on the superhuman. Completing a class in Denver before Christmas, he received a wire to report to Los Angeles on the morning of January 1 to begin a new class of eight with a string of strange dogs being crated from Morristown. He did so, and in the process managed to meet and fall in love with Lu Dahl, the sister of one of his students. On their honeymoon the following year, he turned over two dogs with students in Gallup, New Mexico. He did countless little odd jobs as well. He had not only papered the old dining room with Gretchen Green, but constructed beautifully scaled relief maps of Morristown with the streets marked in braille, so that the students could study their routes. There were no challenges in a modern instructor's life that were not dwarfed into insignificance by comparison with Debetaz's past.

For Willi Ebeling, The Seeing Eye was not simply a philanthropy, it was a way of life, a religion. He wrote, "The dogs are the soul of our organization. They need to be taught, but at the same time they teach. They drive home the lesson that to be understood is to understand, and because they are the symbol of truth, they demand truth. One must believe this, and one must live it to render the service to which our students are entitled."

Willi himself believed it and lived it, and he expected the instructors to do the same. He worked long hours at one quarter of the salary he could have earned in the business world. So should they. The principal satisfactions of working for The Seeing Eye were not material, but spiritual. His was the philosophy that justifies underpaying ministers and teachers because they are supposed to be idealists who love their work for its own sake.

In the end, Agnes Fowler's fears were justified. In 1950, Robert Lee, whose back was hurting and whose academic background was scientific, left The Seeing Eye for a job in jet engineering. He had been with the school twelve years. In 1951, Curt Weeman, a veteran of seventeen years, went to work as a draftsman. A few months later, a fourteen-year man, Harold Dickerman, and a four-year man, David Evans, also left. In less than two years, The Seeing Eye had lost four instructors with a combined total of forty-seven years' experience. After more than twenty years of recruiting and training apprentices, the school's Achilles' heel was still vulnerable.

CHAPTER 15

Love in
the Lead

ALFREDA GALT, who worked in The Seeing Eye's public relations firm, recalls showing Willi Ebeling some copy she had written for the annual report. As he read, she could see he was uncomfortable. He squirmed restlessly in his desk chair. Finally he looked up with a pained expression.

"It sounds so proud, don't you know," he said. "So proud." He hesitated for a moment, then waved at the walls of his office. "We here are not The Seeing Eye, don't you know. The Seeing Eye is not the staff or the building. The Seeing Eye is the graduates out in the field."

Through his extensive correspondence with the graduates, Willi Ebeling was acutely aware of the challenges that confronted them. That first walk at home alone was a test. A roommate at the school told me that on his first solo back home, he struck his head on a steel beam projecting from the back of a truck and had to have eight stitches. The experience could have been traumatic, shaking his confidence fatally, but he had been well schooled and he kept the faith.

John Gates of Artesia, New Mexico, wrote Willi Ebeling of an experience typical of the novice first trying his wings: "I was approaching the railroad track here about the third week home, when I heard an oncoming train I had not realized was so near. Terror seized my exploding brain as the train bore down upon us, and while my impulse was to break and run, mentally I could hear my instructor shouting, 'Follow your dog!', so follow I did, expecting to be hamburger at any moment. Then I realized the engine had passed in front of us. Dodie and I were still walking briskly, and no one was dead. I stopped and planted a big kiss on Dodie's cold nose."

The jealousy of a new graduate's spouse could wreck the partnership of dog and master. Two weeks after leaving L'Oeil Qui Voit, the dog of a French veteran arrived at the Vevey railroad station with no word of explanation. The dog had enabled the old soldier to resume an independent social life. Leaving his wife at home, he went to the café to hobnob with his cronies. Resenting his freedom, his wife had sent the dog back.

A similar scenario has been repeated several times at the American Seeing Eye. The wife of one of my classmates told my wife she liked having a blind husband she could "keep around the house." Three weeks after graduation, his dog came back on the pretext it was "unclean."

The mother of a teenaged boy, Miner Clites, was more generous about his dog, Joy. "One evening, he didn't appear for dinner. I finally located him by telephoning around to his friends. When he came home, I sputtered and scolded and said the dog would go back, if I had to hunt him for his meals. But sputtering was all, because he got a kick out of it. Joy couldn't go out of his life now. Honestly, I got a lump in my throat, and I got a real thrill out of the fact that he could go out and be late for dinner, like other mothers' sons." When Miner Clites returned for his second dog, Willi Ebeling was delighted to find that the gangling adolescent weighing 120 pounds had filled out into a young man of 170 pounds, who "laid it to being able to get out and exercise after I got Joy."

Family, friends, and the public at large had to be

taught to keep hands off a graduate working his dog. Edward Hoffman's friends had nearly ruined Helga by pulling her master one way while she was trying to lead him another. A dog who is wearing a harness is on duty, working or not, and should never be patted or spoken to. A graduate who had ignored this rule came back to The Seeing Eye during my first class. He had allowed strangers to pat his dog so indiscriminately that she continually whined for attention and was a public nuisance in public places. Back at the school, he stubbornly disclaimed any responsibility for having spoiled his dog and was sent home without her.

It is not easy to convince the average American that other people's dogs are not to be patted, but Jack Humphrey made a telling point with a woman on the bus going back to the school. Shortly after she had leaned down to pat a dog in training at his feet, he reached over and patted her knee. Stiffening with outrage, she gasped, "How dare you! I don't know you."

"No," Jack shot back, "and you don't know my dog."

Occasionally graduates try to work under conditions that are too much for a dog to handle. A young woman who lived in Brooklyn took a job in Trenton that required her to commute three hours each way. Her dog became extremely nervous, and the school advised her either to move closer to her work or find employment closer to home.

Some graduates found that their dogs were too much to handle. Agnes Stone, a diminutive braille teacher, was paired with a shepherd who pulled right out of her grasp to chase squirrels. The problem was solved by retraining Miss Stone with a Weimaraner better suited to her size and strength. On at least one occasion, a male graduate found that his Doberman was too much dog for him. He went to the park one day with a sandwich lunch for himself and a beef knuckle for his guide. He had finished his lunch before the dog had fairly begun on the bone. Moreover, he made it clear he had no intention of leaving it. The man was marooned on the park bench for two hours while his Doberman gnawed on the knuckle.

Rosa Buchko reported behavior in her dog that defied analysis at long distance, and Debetaz was sent to observe her on a walk. Half a block from her apartment, her dog had to pass an organ grinder with a monkey on a string. In the wink of an eye, the monkey was on the dog's back— to the distress of the dog, the mystification of Rosa, and the amusement of the passing Yahoos. Since nothing could be done about the monkey's owner, Rosa had to be retrained with a more spirited dog, one who knew how to get a monkey off its back.

In a few instances the school had reports of graduates begging with dogs. Most of these were false. The beggars were not Seeing Eye graduates. Some were not even blind. But a Seeing Eye dog had to be taken from a man in Phila-delphia, and on another occasion Morris Frank reclaimed the dog of a young woman who was attending a school for beggars in Chicago. Twice the threat of recalling dogs spurred their owners to find gainful employment.

Regularly, Willi Ebeling received letters or phone calls from students having difficulties. Harold Rosenthal called one day in a panic because Prancer refused to walk down a certain street. Willi explained that he must have corrected her unjustly on that street, and now she was avoiding it because she was afraid it might happen again. Rosenthal wrote him afterwards, "Your suggestion was that I walk down that street and, if necessary, get down on my knees and try to talk her out of it. And do you know, Mr. Ebeling? I literally did just that—with success."

With his passionate faith in dogs, it was emotionally impossible for Willi Ebeling to admit that they were ever in the wrong. The master must always be somehow at fault. But today Debetaz, Myrose, and other experienced instruc-tors recognize that the problem may lie in the peculiar chemistry of dog and master for which neither is at fault.

Dogs actually suffer psychosomatic illnesses from mismatings. When recalled to the school and paired with different masters, their health problems miraculously disappear, while their former masters have no difficulties with new dogs.

What can be difficult for masters to grasp is that every dog is an individual. All seven of my dogs have been shepherds, all taught to do the same job by the same methods, yet all endowed with their distinct personalities and idiosyncrasies. Because the relationship between dog and master is so intimate, these individual differences can be bothersome. Debetaz used to warn returning students that comparing a second dog to the first was as dangerous as comparing a second spouse to the first, but it is difficult to avoid. Minnie, my first dog, was a hard puller and so fast that, in all our years together on the Princeton campus, I was never passed except by someone at a run. Wick, though he was much taller and rangier, ambled along at a slower pace and with much less pull. It took time, patience, and concentration to adjust.

Some graduates seem unable to make the emotional investment required to achieve full partnership with a dog. Yet the emotional investment, the ability to give fully of yourself to your dog, to confide your whole trust, and to show your concern and affection is even more important than physical coordination or a sense of orientation. Emil Buchko, Rosa's husband, dwarfed in stature and so lame when he arrived at the school that he had to depend on his dog's strength to pull him up the curbs, proved to be an excellent worker, and was able to write the following letter:

> During the war, I was commuting to New York City and working in a defense plant. I was coming up the subway stairs from the Long Island subway to Grand Central Station proper, when a man offered me assistance. I said no thank you. I had just a few minutes to walk through the station to make my train. Going down the first ramp, another man approached me and said, "May I assist you, sir?"

Not pausing to reply because of time, I said, "No thank you. I know where I'm going."

This did not seem to satisfy the two men following me. I could hear one say to the other, "I wonder how he knows where he is going?"

I turned my head slightly while still walking with Gulpin and said, "Don't worry. My dog reads the signs."

Little did I realize these men would take me so seriously. When I reached the main concourse of the lower level, Gulpin turned into a gate marked Track 116. Behind me I heard one man mutter, "I'll be g—d d——ed!"

There seems no end to what a well-adjusted dog can do for its master. On his second trip to San Francisco, Debetaz was at first mystified to find that the dogs of his first class never made a mistake in boarding the correct trolley cars to take their masters to and from work. He concluded that they identified them by smells characteristic of the quarters of the city through which they ran. When my wife and I were unsure where we had parked the car in a big lot, I would turn the problem over to Missie, who always went straight to the car without hesitation.

On the occasion of his retirement from The Seeing Eye after twenty-five years, Willi Ebeling received literally hundreds of letters from graduates. Passages from them will give an idea of the extraordinary range and variety in the lives of Seeing Eye graduates and their dogs.

Maxine Hansen, whose work took her all over the state of Wisconsin, wrote: "In our life of almost continual travel, Pansy never forgets which is our hotel room, nor where the hotel is when we have left it. Wherever we have left our things is home, and she always knows where home is. The lapse of time means nothing. Having been there once, she can recognize the place any length of time later. I wish someone could tell me how a dog can remember that way."

Munroe Fox's dog allowed him to commune with nature in the country around Albuquerque: "Missy has made it possible for me to spend long quiet hours alone fishing in some lake, secure in the knoweldge that I have a faithful pair of eyes to guide me back to camp and that I need ask the aid of no man to enjoy the quiet and solitude of our lovely mountains."

Thousands of miles away in New York City, Harman Gainer lived in anything but solitude. "Sarge knows every subway entrance and exit that I use in my daily work as a salesman. He finds a seat for me in the subway and the buses that I use each day. He knows at my command when to go to the change booth or when to go through the turnstiles of the subway station. He knows every building and office that I go into."

Jennings Lattimer's Fran was a great help to him in his work as a piano tuner. "We have been visiting all the 130 Pittsburgh public schools periodically, keeping their pianos in good repair. Fran soon learned to know her pianos, too. When I walk into a schoolroom, and she gets her eyes on a piano, she takes me straight to it. This is a big help, for we often go early in the morning before the teachers arrive, as that is when we can work without being disturbed. As soon as I begin putting my tools together, she is up and ready to go. In the school washroom, she takes me straight to the washbowl. I can leave my coat in one room, go to several others rooms to work, and then when I tell her, 'Get my coat,' she will almost invariably go straight to it."

Ralph Stewart from Salt Lake City felt some uncertainty about Rollo in the beginning. "I worried about having Rollo guide me and my wife, who is also blind, uptown for the first time, but he did a super job of taking us, and he is working out wonderfully. The only trouble I have with the big lug, he loves stealing kiddies' ice-cream cones. He is so big that he sticks his head over their shoulders and slurp, it is gone, all unknown to me until I hear a scream. Then it is too late, and I have to pay for his fun, but he wags his tail and is so pleased with himself that I haven't the heart to scold him."

Henry and Mary Driskell were a blind couple from Chicago who each had a dog. She wrote Willi Ebeling, "If you could be here in Chicago when the four of us start out from home, you would see Mr. Driskell and Muffer speeding on a way ahead, and Una and me coming along behind as fast as we can. We're still slower than they are. Of course, Muffer always stops at the end of each block and looks back to see if Una is coming all right. Folks tell us it looks as if she were looking out for her little sister.

"In our home, Una and Muffer would put on one of their boxing matches for you. They get out in the middle of the room and tumble and box each other and expect much praise and rooting from their audience. I might add they do stop the show instantly when we give the command."

When Mrs. John Stern had her baby, Val became more than a guide. "For instance, when the baby was still quite tiny and lying in her bassinet, she would throw her rattle to the floor. Without a word from me, Val would walk over to the rattle, pick it up, place it in my hand, and curl up to go back to sleep until she again heard the rattle hit the floor. The baby is now a little over a year old. Val picks up toys that are out of her reach and takes them to her."

Dogs adapted themselves to a variety of professions. C. L. Finch's Trooper made himself at home in the courtroom.

After graduating from The Seeing Eye, Trooper and I opened a law office in Antigo, Wisconsin. One day when I was presenting a case, the judge interrupted me. "Mr. Finch, all during this trial, your dog has been sitting beside you holding a glove, a dollar bill, and a document in his mouth. Do these things have any bearing on the case?" I explained that Trooper was only doing his job, picking up after his untidy master.

Trooper almost had his own day in court. I had a phone call from the sheriff one morning. "Mr. Finch, is Trooper in your office?" I thought he was. After looking under my desk, I replied, "His leash is here, but he isn't."

"Well," came the dry voice of the sheriff, "he's up here at the county jail. I just booked him on a charge of lewd and lascivious behavior on the courthouse lawn. He wants you to spring him and his girl friend."

Dr. Jack Wilcox got his Ph.D. in clinical psychiatry at Michigan:

> King's calmness and imperturbability are his outstanding traits. This has turned out to be a very fortunate circumstance in my work. I have worked with him in mental hospitals where I might at any time run into disturbed patients who make all sorts of approaches to him. Even when their behavior is what might be considered threatening by most dogs, King pays absolutely no attention and calmly concentrates on taking me where I want to go.
>
> He also makes himself inconspicuous when a patient comes to the office, and only once in all my experience have I had a patient sufficiently frightened by him to make it necessary to put him in another room. Very often his presence is a definite contribution to a patient who finds it difficult to talk. Almost all of them have a dog story that comes to mind and furnishes a beginning topic for conversation.

In the IBM laboratory in upstate New York, Dr. Glaser's Pal found his preoccupation with computers boring. "I am sure she sometimes thinks human beings are demented creatures. One particular activity that is necessary from time to time is the plugging of wires into the control panels of the IBM machine. The first time I occupied myself with this ridiculous conduct, Pal became perturbed. It seemed futile to her to spend so much time placing the ends of wires in small holes in a useless piece of plastic. However, her training and good manners came through, and now if I drop a wire, she will pick it up for me and put it in my lap."

The key to all these adaptations is the praise that makes it clear to the dog that their masters appreciate what they are doing. Work then becomes a pleasure. Don Faith reported Otis's reaction to construction work in Chicago.

They now have the midway torn up, and they are installing lights at the intersection. This makes it necessary for Otis to make a detour, which the average person would consider a bother. Otis, however, looks forward to this detour work and regards it as a challenge which he truly enjoys meeting. Whenever he comes to the barricade, he pulls with that sure, steady eagerness of one who enjoys his work, yet knows its every intricate detail. He then has to pause to peer around a tar truck to see if anything is coming. After we listen to the traffic, I give the command of forward, and we proceed across the street.

Because of the difficulty of the barricade plus a blocking truck, I give a strong reward. Sometimes, this is taken by Otis as a matter of course, but every once in a while, he has to stop and lift his big shaggy head up to my right hand and lick it as if to say, 'Aren't I the smartest person you ever saw?'

We have all experienced the contagion of a dog's pleasure in a challenge. On her first trip through Philadelphia's Thirtieth Street Station, my present dog Hessa seemed to swell with pride, and I had the distinct impression that she was walking down the exact center of the room looking with regal interest from side to side. An earlier dog, Sally, spent five years with me in the solitary life of a writer, before I took a job that required me to fly 50,000 miles a year. One two-week trip took us to Pittsburgh, Cincinnati, Chicago, Omaha, San Francisco, Portland, Seattle, Los Angeles, Minneapolis, St. Paul, and New York. I was in a different hotel almost every night. That meant that Sally's "parks" were constantly changing, but she ate, emptied, found her way in and out of hotels, elevators, restaurants, and offices, followed passenger-service representatives through airports as though she had a radar fix on them, and was always ready to wag her tail at a word of praise.

Genevieve Wiley described her Rene's response to a different sort of challenge:

> Four years ago, the city was making extensive repairs for a number of blocks along our main thoroughfare here in Pasadena, putting in a complete new set of pipes. After two weeks, the day came when I was to have my hair done. I heard machinery in the distance, but decided to go on.
>
> I soon found myself right in the midst of the work which was plenty noisy. Rene was on the outside, the side of the machinery, but aside from slowing up a little, she kept steadily on her way. One of the workmen shouted that the dog was doing fine, but I noticed that she kept pushing me very close to the buildings, almost against them. When I reached the shop and mentioned the way we had come, everyone was simply horrified. All along the block where Rene had kept me so close to the buildings was just a narrow strip of sidewalk. The rest was a great hole where pipes were being laid.

Several graduates have had narrow escapes. Albert Korp lived five miles outside Grand Junction, Colorado. "I decided one day to go into town, and while walking along a country road, Queenie turned sharp, took me across the ditch, and never stopped until we were against the fence. By that time I heard something coming down the road. It was about fifty head of rodeo horses that were being driven by some men I knew. They told me they saw what happened. Without the training of Queenie, I would have been trampled by the horses, because they could not stop them or get to me in any way." Ray Coffey of Lenore, South Carolina, had his adventures with Pram:

> One day I went up to Collettsville in Caldwell County to visit an uncle. Pram and I got off the bus on the main highway and took a road leading to my uncle's home. When we got to a bridge over a stream of water on this road, Pram

stopped. I talked to him, but he would not go a step farther. I knew something was wrong.

We turned back and went to a store nearby where I had
a cousin working. The cousin took us in his truck back to
the bridge. He found that two planks were missing, making
a space wide enough for me to fall into the water below.

In 1952, Pram showed an unusual alertness for my safety.
We were riding home in a bus. Without any warning, Pram
jumped from the seat and started with me for the door.
When we reached the door, the driver announced the bus
was on fire and ordered all passengers off. Pram and I were
the first passengers off the burning bus, because he was the
first to know the danger.

City life held its dangers, too. George Cohen and
Bambi

were caught at a busy intersection in Montreal at a time
when some bank robbers were trying to make a getaway.
We were crossing the street at a traffic light when some
shots rang out. At first, I thought it was some leftover fireworks, but I felt Bambi freeze against my legs, blocking
my path.

I realized something serious was wrong, when she took
the lead firmly and jaywalked as fast as she could through
the cars across to the other corner and into a doorway. I
knew it must be serious if she would break one of the
strictest rules of her training by cutting through traffic. Her
quick thinking in pulling me into that doorway almost
assuredly saved me from what might have been serious
injury. At almost the exact spot where we had been standing, a Royal Canadian Mounted Police pursuing the robbers was shot and killed.

Ethel Stevens and Heidi operated a candy stand in a
New Haven hospital. On her way home one evening, she
was stopped and told

of a shooting in a theater and that one of the bandits was
hiding only two buildings from where we stood. My first
thought was to return to the hospital, but I learned that

all streets in that direction were blocked, while the police looked for the second bandit around that way. I had no alternative but to command, "Heidi, forward." Heidi appeared to be thinking for a minute or two. Then she turned, retraced her steps to Broad Street, turned left and waited for a policeman to allow us to cross. We then proceeded for a full block to High Street. Here, amid police whistles, automobiles, and pedestrians, she turned a sharp left and worked her way two blocks and then right in the direction of home. When we passed the leading hotel, a shot was fired. One of the bandits had killed himself. People and police were everywhere, but Heidi walked steadily forward to the bus stop. By the time we reached the bus stop, she was sniffling hard and rubbing her face against my coat. My eyes were watering and burning, too, for we had walked two blocks through where tear bombs were used. Until now, Heidi was most calm, but now that we were safe from danger, she began to tremble a great deal. All evening she was very nervous, but the next morning, she was as usual.

Edward LeMoine wrote a letter printed in the September 1964 issue of *The Guide*:

Lina and I had just boarded the bus when the rain started. Thirty minutes later we stepped off the bus into several inches of water. By the time we had gone three blocks, it was up to my ankles on the sidewalk and nearly to my knees crossing the street, as the water poured down from higher ground.

Crossing the third street, the water came almost to my hips. Lina, it seemed to me, must actually be swimming, but she slowed down perceptibly at the point where she calculated the curb should be and, so help me, it was. We went another block in water up to Lina's chest, and she again found the curb down, but only after she showed me a low-hanging tree branch. I lifted it, and we passed under unscathed. We crossed the street in somewhat unorthodox fashion, angling to the left away from the intersection and almost directly to the house of my friend, where I was expected for dinner. When we reached the porch, I leaned down to hug and praise her, and she was all over me, licking my face and emitting little squeaks of joy. All through our ordeal, I had talked to her in a calm voice and encouraged her frequently with "Hopp, hopp. That's a good girl." We knew we needed each other to get through safely. With this kind of understanding and love, we could go anyplace.

The important point of these stories is not their melodrama, but their illustration of the partnerships, the sense of needing each other, for Lisa and Heidi and Bambi were heartened by knowing that their humans trusted them, spoke to them calmly and encouragingly, and followed the signals they gave through their harness handles. People do not go to The Seeing Eye in the hope of being rescued from rodeo horses, burning buses, bank robbers or flash floods, but for freedom of movement.

Jeanne Pechtel remarked, "People are so often disappointed when they expectantly ask if Nell has ever saved my life and I answer no. Oh, of course, she has got me out of the way of backing trucks, but it is for the freedom to be in such situations that I am grateful to Nellie. A guide dog's business after all, is not rescue, but safety maintenance. It is the certainty that she will keep me out of situations from which I would need rescuing that makes it possible for me to cross unstoplighted busy streets, to catch an el in a rained-on, rush-hour mob, or for that matter to run in fluffy new snow."

I remember taking Sally to the Boston Common to empty one day. We were crossing the sidewalk to Sally's accustomed stretch of grass, when a truck bore down on us, and I obeyed Sally's sudden check without even thinking. If I had been walking with a cane instead of a dog, I could doubtless have heard the truck, but I would have had to be listening, alert, tense with concentration. With a dog, I had the freedom to relax, think of other things, and to let Sally be my eyes and ears.

There is emotional support in the partnership of a dog that is an inestimable asset. In January 1942, when I sought readmission to Princeton with Minnie, I met unexpected opposition. I thought the matter had been settled before I went to The Seeing Eye, but suddenly the college authorities were telling me that I ought to spend six months to two years in a school for the blind first. In effect, they wanted me to "learn to be blind." I pled my case passionately, but I am not sure I could have prevailed if I had been pleading only for myself. I was pleading for Minnie, too, or rather for our partnership. If we were to succeed, we needed the meaningful challenge of my return to Princeton. My deep-seated conviction of this made that return inevitable.

Other graduates have experienced this same sense of reinforcement. Gabe Fuqua was discontentedly running a candy stand in Jackson, Mississippi, when he heard a radio interview of Hamilton Jenkins in Chicago. Jenkins, a black former middleweight boxer, was returning to Denver with his second Seeing Eye dog. This insipred Fuqua to go to Morristown to get his own dog, Xon, and that led him still further. He wrote Willi Ebeling, "Xon and I went to school this summer at the College of Swedish Masseurs in Chicago. I had never been to a place as large as Chicago in my life before. A friend wanted to know if I'd be afraid, and I said, 'Afraid of what? Xon and I can go anywhere anyone else can go.'

"So off we go to Chicago. We didn't know anyone there, but before three nights were up, Xon and I had many a new friend. Now I have a good job at the Jackson Y.M.C.A. Health Club as a masseur, but I know in my heart, had it not been for Xon, I would never have had the courage to make the grade."

But Xon would not let him stop there. As Fuqua recalled later, "Xon lit a fire in me and opened new doors I only dreamed about before. I went back to school and completed college and law school. Now I am a member of the

Mississippi Bar Association and a justice of the peace." The courage and confidence that Xon's love inspired led Fuqua from behind a candy stand to membership in the Mississippi Bar as surely as her harness handle guided him through the streets of Jackson.

A few months ago, I was having lunch in New York with a friend, and when we rose to go, I somehow failed to pick up Hessa's leash. This was a gesture so instinctive after nearly forty years that I am at a loss to explain the lapse. My companion and I were walking toward the door when I felt something against my left leg. It was Hessa walking exactly where she should have been, at heel. I might forget —how could I have!—but she was there, loyal, loving, trustful. The love of a Seeing Eye dog is a pearl beyond all price, and so is the love for a Seeing Eye dog. It has filled the hearts and minds of thousands of blind men and women and given them the courage to do what would have been impossible without it. Their mutual love leads them both. That love is the heart of The Seeing Eye.

CHAPTER 16

A New
Approach

"I KNEW I could never replace Uncle Willi," George Werntz recalled long afterward. "Gosh! No one could. That guy was one of a kind. But Henry Colgate thought we needed a new approach."

Henry Colgate became president of The Seeing Eye on the death of Dorothy Eustis in the fall of 1946, and it was he who brought in George Werntz to replace Willi Ebeling. A few years earlier, circumstances had seemed to indicate a different successor.

Dorothy's younger son, Harrison, had taken an active interest in The Seeing Eye at an early age. When the school was reincorporated in New Jersey in 1932, he was both an incorporator and a trustee at the age of eighteen. Even before that, he had worked with dogs at L'Oeil Qui Voit. Later he was able to work dogs under blindfold. After he graduated from Harvard in 1936, he took a job working on membership enrollments with Marian Jobson of Hartwell, Jobson, and Kibbee. Both Marian and Debby assumed that Harrison was being groomed for a position at The Seeing Eye, ultimately as Willi Ebeling's successor. He was highly intelligent, personable, and sensitive and would have been a logical choice. But in the spring of 1938, while he was still working for Hartwell, Jobson, and Kibbee, Harrison Wood contracted a fatal illness.

Dorothy Eustis accompanied him on his last trip to Europe that summer. Harrison died in Switzerland in September. It was a terrible blow to Dorothy. When she returned to America, instead of going back to the gatehouse in Whippany, she withdrew to her New York apartment. It is likely she had meant to reduce her involvement in The Seeing Eye in any case. The board of trustees had been expanded, and since 1936 Henry Colgate had been serving as chairman. Her active leadership was no longer crucial, but if Harrison had lived, he would have been a strong emotional tie. As it was, her withdrawal to New York removed a vital presence from the grounds at Whippany.

It was the first of a series of changes. The newly married Debetazes moved into Dorothy's gatehouse apartment. When Jack Humphrey went into the Coast Guard, the Myroses took over the ground floor. Dickson Hartwell, who had just completed *Dogs Against Darkness*, the first history of The Seeing Eye, was off to the war, and Marian Jobson, who carried on the firm with Margaret Kibbee, was elected a vice president.

Following the war, there were further changes. Aunt Mary Campbell retired in 1945. The death of Dorothy Eustis in 1946 virtually coincided with the elevation of Ibby Hutchinson to vice president of the division for the blind and Debby Debetaz to vice president of the training division. The income from memberships was so much in excess of expenditures that Marian Jobson was instructed to slacken the pace of enrollment, but legacies continued to swell the school's net worth. It surpassed $2,500,000 in 1948 and continued to grow despite a number of capital expenditures.

New training kennels had been constructed on the Whippany property in 1945. In 1948, the breeding stock was moved into kennels on a 100-acre tract purchased in nearby Mendham. The isolation of the breeding stock from the dogs in training was designed to free it from the contagious diseases that handicapped the program at Whippany. John Weagley, who had been specially educated on Seeing Eye scholarships at Rutgers, took charge of the breeding farm.

In 1950, the school opened a woman's wing. There had been a relative scarcity of women students in the thirties. Now they were a growing minority, and the "harem" gave the school the capacity to house 240 students a year. A record number of 187 students graduated in 1950, but the most important event of the year was the appointment of Willi Ebeling's assistant and eventual successor.

After graduating from Colgate in 1933, George Werntz, Jr., taught for four years at Irving, a private boys' school in Tarrytown, New York. When Henry Colgate had inquired at the university for a likely undergraduate to act as a sort of companion and athletic coach for his sons during the summer, young George had taken the job and spent several summers with the Colgates at Lake Placid. In 1937, when the Irving School became defunct, he got a job in the admissions office at Colgate and became its director just one month before being called into the navy in 1942, where he spent three and a half years as personnel officer on the staff of the commander of the Air Force Pacific Fleet. Returning to Colgate after the war as a lieutenant in the Naval Reserve, he became assistant dean.

In physique. background, mind-set, and, most of all, in style, George Werntz was very unlike the man he was to succeed. Willi was short, slight, and wiry. George was tall, broad-shouldered, and muscular. Both men were conservative, but whereas Willi's mind was intuitive and mercurial, George's was rational and pedestrian in the sense that it moved logically from step to step. Willi had come from the business world; George's background was almost entirely academic. It was natural for him to term Debetaz "dean of the faculty," while Ibby Hutchinson was "director of admissions and dean of students." Willi Ebeling governed

The Seeing Eye with the intensity of the zealous abbot of a medieval monastery. George Werntz gave off the aura of the congenial headmaster of a boys' preparatory school.

He began work on August 1 and spent nearly three and a half years as Willi's assistant. Under Debetaz, he learned the technique of guide dog instruction, personally trained two dogs, and adjusted them to a pair of students. In Marian Jobson's New York office, he worked on every phase of education, extension, and membership enrollment. By the time he took over as executive vice president on January 1, 1954, he had a thorough grounding in all the school's programs as they had been in the past, but Henry Colgate was calling for a new approach.

George describes it this way: "Willi always used to say that if we built a better mousetrap, the world would beat a path to our door, but Mr. Colgate felt we should be improving that path ourselves." This was basically a problem in public relations, and The Seeing Eye had three problem areas.

The first concerned the attitude of workers for the blind toward guide dogs. Willi Ebeling had long since patched up his quarrel with Herbert Immeln, and as Seeing Eye graduates began to occupy positions of importance in various agencies, the school won friends; but there were still a number of workers who were hostile for one reason or another. Blind people who went to The Seeing Eye came back changed. They withdrew from sheltered workshops to take better-paying jobs in industry or business. With their newfound freedom, they had less need for the agencies, and agency workers did not like feeling unneeded. Many counselors secretly feared, disliked, or distrusted dogs, and advised their clients against them. Others envied The Seeing Eye its spectacular financial success and sought to minimize its achievements.

A second problem stemmed from the continuing proliferation of guide-dog schools. With the exception of Leader Dogs in Rochester, Michigan, and Guide Dogs for the Blind in San Rafael, California, their output was insignificant, but they competed for philanthropic dollars with other agencies, confused the public, and produced substandard dogs. Returning graduates reported that after accounts of the deaths of their old dogs appeared in the papers, representatives of other schools wrote or telephoned to offer them replacements free of charge and even promised to pay full transportation.

More pressing than either the hostility of agency workers or fly-by-night guide-dog schools was what George Werntz labeled "The Seeing Eye's Number-One Public Relations Problem." In a memorandum addressed to the board on August 1, 1954, he drew attention to the increasingly embarrassing awareness of the school's net worth, which had surpassed $4,500,000 in the previous fiscal year, and which grew annually because annual income exceeded expenditures by a wide margin. Under these circumstances, it was difficult to justify asking for membership contributions. The National Information Bureau, a private nonprofit corporation which monitors philanthropic fund raising for interested contributors, was becoming highly critical.

One way of decreasing the surplus was to increase expenditures. In 1954 the school hired a resident nurse to monitor the health of the growing number of diabetics attending classes. George also arranged to have a Morristown doctor come to the school to examine diabetic students on the first or second day of class. But expenses of this kind were a mere drop in the bucket, and Werntz proposed to the board several options involving sizeable outlays of money. One was the establishment of a program to make grants to related philanthropies. A second was the opening of a branch school in another part of the country. A third stemmed from the second.

It would be foolish to open a branch school for which there was no need. There were many divergent estimates of the number of blind people capable of and interested in using guide dogs, but there was no scientific information on the subject. In true academic fashion, Werntz proposed that The Seeing Eye use a substantial part of its surplus to finance a thoroughgoing scientific survey of the demand for guide dogs, to be conducted by a competent outside organization. The board of trustees responded enthusiastically, and in due course, the School of Social Work at Columbia University was chosen. Scholars there were selected to design the study, which would require a large team of social workers to conduct personal interviews with a sample population of 500 blind men and women. It would cost some $250,000 and take several years to complete. Pending the outcome, the board would make no decision regarding a branch school.

In the interim, George devoted himself to improving relations with other agencies. Unlike Uncle Willi, who loathed meetings, he was a good mixer. He participated actively in conventions of the A.A.W.B., where he enjoyed the old-school tie spirit of the annual reunion breakfast with Seeing Eye graduates. Accompanied by Ibby Hutchinson, he attended other conferences where he made a good impression on several agency executives who had felt, with some justification, that Willi Ebeling looked down on them.

In 1956, George's efforts bore fruit. On the recommendation of the Texas Commission for the Blind, a committee studying the advisability of founding a guide-dog school in Texas came to The Seeing Eye. George described the study in progress, expressed his doubt as to the need for another school, and pointed out that since The Seeing Eye now paid all travel costs above fifty dollars per student, Morristown was within the financial reach of blind Texans. (After 1960, The Seeing Eye would pay full travel costs.) The committee was dissuaded from founding another school.

At about the same time, a New York legislative investigation of "charity rackets" uncovered the scandalous fact that a professional fund raiser had raised $57,000 for an organization called Guiding Eyes for the Blind, which had never supplied a guide dog to a blind person, never trained a dog for guide work, and never employed a guide-dog instructor. Exposés of this kind hurt The Seeing Eye by association, but worse was to come. Behind George Werntz's back, Guiding Eyes succeeded in hiring away Edward Fouser, an instructor with eleven years' experience at The Seeing Eye and junior only to Debetaz and Myrose. Of nearly seventy-five men apprenticed over the years, only six remained at The Seeing Eye. Six others were working for rival organizations; one of them, Harold Dickerman, was at Double-A Guiding Dogs, founded in Wisconsin only the year before.

On April 25, 1956, the twenty-eighth anniversary of his arrival at Vevey in 1928, Morris Frank retired from the school he had founded. From the beginning he had served as The Seeing Eye's roving ambassador, traveling literally hundreds of thousands of miles across the United States and Canada. Since his marriage in 1942, his wife Lois had frequently accompanied him. In 1954, they had completed a three-year program of travel, interviewing 300 ophthalmologists and a majority of The Seeing Eye's graduates in all forty-eight states and Canada. They had been on the road for eighteen of thirty-six months. Enough was enough. Morris felt he had done all he could for the school. It was time to move on. As he had once demonstrated that a guide dog was a safe and effective travel aid, he now wanted to prove that a blind man could be a success in business. At forty-eight, he launched his own insurance agency in an office at 10 Park Place North in the center of Morristown.

To succeed Morris, George chose a very different sort of man. The thirties required a brash young rebel like Morris to break down barriers, but times had changed. Now the need was for diplomacy. Robert Whitstock was a graduate of Hamilton College and Harvard Law School who had received his first dog, Nesta, in 1952. Bob was soft-spoken and articulate, clear-thinking and deliberate. There is no greater proof of the respect he inspired in his fellow workers than that they would ultimately elect him president of the A.A.W.B.

A valuable supplement to Bob Whitstock's fieldwork was financed by another of those windfalls that were the school's number-one public relations problem. A legacy provided a sizeable fund for Seeing Eye publications, and in 1957, it paid for a revised and handsomely illustrated version of *The Newly Blind* under the title *If Blindness Occurs*. It was widely circulated to hospital staffs, social and rehabilitation workers, and other groups whom Bob addressed in the course of his travels.

In the fall of 1957, George Werntz planned an innovation in alumni relations. Members of the staff would make a long-playing Christmas record to be sent to all graduates. Familiar voices would send season's greetings and inform them of recent developments with an immediacy of impact far beyond any letter.

The Christmas record was a triumphant success and only the first of many, but while it was still in its planning stage, George received word of the death of Henry Colgate on October 12. It brought an end to more than twenty years of his productive service and leadership, and George was saddened by the loss of his long-time friend and patron, but he was fortunate in the election of his successor. James Carey, a vice president of the Bank of New York, had for many years been the treasurer of The Seeing Eye. He assumed the presidency of the school at a most difficult stage in the solution of its public relations problems.

As George Werntz had anticipated, the National Information Bureau had become strident in its objections to an organization with assets that now exceeded $10 million continuing to raise funds for its annual operating budget. Jim Carey and George Werntz proposed to appease the National Information Bureau and court public favor with a two-pronged solution. The Seeing Eye would set up a program of grants to philanthropies in related fields and extend all memberships for one year without asking for contributions. To the conservative Wall Street financiers on the board, this seemed a form of fiscal madness, and it required all the persuasiveness Jim Carey could muster to win board approval. As it was, the grants program was inaugurated with a gift of $30,000 to the Retina Foundation, which was working for the prevention of blindness, and the Seeing Eye membership was informed that, as of October 1, 1959, no contributions would be needed in the year ahead. The response to this unprecedented action bordered on the ecstatic. Letters poured in to congratulate The Seeing Eye on its enlightened policy and to promise renewed support as soon as it was needed. This public approbation and the reassuring fact that, even without membership contributions, legacies continued to increase the school's net worth fully convinced the board. On June 1, 1959, it voted to extend memberships without contributions indefinitely.

In the meantime, George Werntz had taken a step that would have been unthinkable for Willi Ebeling. Uncle Willi had encountered so many unscrupulous opportunists and downright frauds in the guide-dog movement that he was highly suspicious. For him, former Seeing Eye apprentices or instructors came under two headings: either they had failed to meet Seeing Eye standards, like Donaldson and Johns, and were incompetent, or they had gone over to the enemy, like Dickerman and Fouser, and were traitors. In either case, he wanted nothing to do with them.

George had a different perspective: "Having been in the educational field, where we had things like the Headmaster's Association and meetings where we could let down our hair and exchange ideas, it always seemed very strange to me that there was no framework for cooperation between the various guide-dog schools."

The preliminary findings of the survey on the demand for guide dogs had given him additional food for thought. It indicated that "the primary reservoir" of potential guide-dog users was only about 1 percent of the legally blind population. This reservoir included an estimated 3,270 persons who combined sufficient motivation with the mental and physical capacity to learn to use guide dogs successfully. Of this number, only a little more than one in eight, or 425 persons, could be expected to apply for dogs within the next year. The Seeing Eye, Leader Dogs for the Blind, and Guide Dogs for the Blind had physical facilities adequate to supply this population with guide dogs. From George's point of view, therefore, these three schools should cooperate in every way to improve standards, expand their programs, and discourage the creation of new schools or the continued existence of those that were substandard.

In 1958, at the initiative and the expense of The Seeing Eye, the leadership of Guide Dogs for the Blind and The Seeing Eye met for a two-day seminar in Denver. Later, George arranged for a similar conference with Leader Dogs in Michigan. In neither case did the schools come to anything like a complete meeting of the minds, but at least an avenue of communication had been opened.

The Demand for Dog Guides by Samuel Finestone, Irving Lukoff, and Martin Whiteman was published in 1960, but The Seeing Eye was familar with its contents long before then. In addition to the primary reservoir of dogs users, there was a secondary reservoir of some 3,400 people who possessed the mental and physical qualifications, but lacked the necessary motivation to use a guide dog. The study also revealed that there was a good deal of misinformation about guide dogs among nonusers.

In view of these findings, George Werntz decided to put more emphasis on the education of potential dog users and their counselors. Accordingly, in August 1959 he employed a second field representative to supplement the work of Bob Whitstock. Miss Norma Farrar was an extremely attractive, bright, and capable young graduate of the University of New Hampshire who had received her first dog in 1953. To gain some exposure on the media of radio and television, Marian Jobson Associates arranged for the taping and filming of a number of public service announcements that emphasized the practical value, public acceptance, and availability of Seeing Eye dogs. Soon after they were shown, their effectiveness was proved by a marked increase in requests for information about The Seeing Eye from potential applicants.

The Jobson office prepared a digest of *The Demand for Dog Guides* and distributed thousands of copies to better business bureaus, chambers of commerce, and rehabilitation agencies. It emphasized that no new guide-dog schools were needed, and it made clear what the school had been stressing ever since Dorothy Eustis reported to the World Congress and A.A.W.B. in 1931: that guide dogs were not for every blind person and that The Seeing Eye had no desire to monopolize the field.

The abandonment of membership enrollments was a real loss, because there had been such an exhilarating esprit de corps among the volunteer workers. They had loved working for The Seeing Eye and missed it. The Jobson office did what it could to keep their interest and enthusiasm alive by continuing to mail copies of the school's quarterly newsletter, *The Guide,* to the entire membership of 15,000. On the positive side, the cessation of fund raising mollified agencies for the blind which had envied The Seeing Eye's success, and the grants program transformed their view of the organization from a potential rival to a potential source of financial support.

The Seeing Eye's new approach was clearly illustrated in its relationship to mobility instructors. As was mentioned earlier, the first systematic study of cane travel occurred during World War II. Dr. Richard E. Hoover designed a light aluminum cane of sufficient length to enable the user to swing it easily from side to side while walking to make certain of safe clearance for each foot as it came forward. Hoover developed methods of teaching the use of his cane, but for some years there were no uniform methods or standards of instruction.

At last, in 1961, Boston College established the first program for mobility instructors to teach the Hoover cane and other travel techniques to the blind. Western Michigan University inaugurated a similar program the following year. In a few years, courses in mobility instruction, or peripatology, would be available in ten colleges and universities, but George Werntz did not wait for this to happen. He realized at once that students from Boston College would go out to teach mobility training at rehabilitation centers and schools in various parts of the country. Now was the time to acquaint them with The Seeing Eye.

In 1962, The Seeing Eye paid all expenses for three Boston College groups, totaling sixteen students with their instructors, to spend two nights and a day in Morristown observing a class in action. Seven students from Western Michigan visited The Seeing Eye on the same basis the same year. From that time forward, The Seeing Eye annually organized and financed workshops for mobility instructors from each of the growing number of college programs.

At such workshops, The Seeing Eye did not proselytize or vaunt the superiority of the dog to the cane. *The Demand for Dog Guides* made it clear that only a small percentage of the blind population could become guide-dog users. The guide dog posed no threat to the cane. As a result, there was no tension. The workshops stimulated a new appreciation of guide dogs, and in time mobility instructors were referring qualified students to The Seeing Eye.

In developing a new approach, George Werntz made an important contribution to The Seeing Eye. He lacked Willi Ebeling's intensity and his incandescent faith in the "truth" symbolized by the dogs. Under George, there was less the sense of being engaged on a religious crusade, but it is neither possible nor desirable to maintain crusading zeal indefinitely. George's style was more relaxed, less despotic than Willi's, Jack's or Dorothy's. Their methods had worked in the thirties, but they were no longer appropriate in the fifties.

As The Seeing Eye entered the sixties, George was making plans for the most ambitious undertaking of his administration, one that would once again expose the school's Achilles' heel.

CHAPTER 17

A Better Mousetrap

THE THIRTY-THIRD annual report of The Seeing Eye contained two special features that contrasted sharply. One was a moving tribute to Willi Ebeling, who had died on December 12, 1961, just thirty years and ten days from the date of the frantic move into The Seeing Eye's first home on the Whippany Road. The other was an exuberant column that looked forward to leaving that home.

A new building was much to be desired. As a result of renovations and additions, the old plant incorporated seven different furnaces in its antiquated heating system. The big house was not fireproof, and the thought of dogs and students trapped on the second floor inspired nightmares. The training kennels had been outgrown, and the office staff was cramped for space.

In 1960, Jim Carey had appointed a long-range planning committee of three trustees, headed by Richard Colgate, who had been elected to the board after the death of his father. The following year, the committee engaged as a consultant Francis Comstock, a Princeton architect. As plans gelled, Comstock was named architect of the new building. For a time, the committee considered building on the old grounds, but an incentive to move was provided by the offer of $250,000 for the school property by the neighboring Bell Laboratories. The committee explored a number of sites before settling on the Kemeys estate, a tract of 120 acres on the Washington Valley Road between Morristown and Mendham. In August 1963, the school agreed to pay $250,000 for the property. Since this was the amount Bell Laboratories was offering for twenty-five acres in Whippany, and the school later sold sixty of the Washington Valley acres for a reservoir, the net result of these real estate transactions was a financial surplus.

The architectural plans were drawn, a contractor was selected, and construction was begun. The cornerstone was laid with all due ceremony on June 5, 1965. The first classes of students entered headquarters in October.

The building was a handsome, red-brick Georgian structure overlooking the Washington Valley. The spacious entrance hall was bisected by a corridor running down the long axis of the building, flanked by offices on either side. At one end was the student wing; at the other, the dining room, kitchen, and a large living room known as the Eustis Lounge. The women were quartered on the ground floor, the men upstairs. The double bedrooms were smaller than those in Whippany, but each had its own bathroom, a decided improvement over the community facilities in the old school.

The construction was fireproof, and the building was air-conditioned—a boon for dogs, students, and staff alike. The recreation rooms were wonderfully spacious. Other features were a separate lounge for instructors, a beautiful outdoor patio, a washing machine and dryer for students' laundry in the basement, an elevator, and a revolving door for teaching purposes. The new building looked like a million dollars, which was its approximate cost, but a number of older students did not like it at first—and I was one of them.

All graduates have an emotional investment in The Seeing Eye, but mine had been unusual. I had written two

books and several articles on the school. I had lectured
about it and discussed it on radio and television programs.
I had grown very fond of Ibby Hutchinson and Uncle
Willi, and I had delivered the eulogy for him at his memo-
rial service. In short, I had become a "true believer," and
true believers are never long on tolerance.

I developed a prejudice against the new building
years before I entered it. My resentment dates from hearing
a recording of the cornerstone laying ceremonies, part of
the annual Christmas record in 1965. The speeches seemed
to me all wrong. Their emphasis was on bricks and mortar.
Their tone was triumphant. As Uncle Willi might have
said, they were "too proud."

Listening to the record, I wanted to shout back that
that building was not The Seeing Eye. The real Seeing
Eye was the dogs, Uncle Willi's symbol of truth. In the
account of the planning and construction of the building,
all sorts of people were named, recognized, and praised:
various trustees, the real estate agent, the architect, the contractor, and everyone, it seemed to me, but the dogs. Except for the dog collar that was cemented into the
cornerstone, there was hardly a reference to the dogs who
were the soul of the enterprise. The Seeing Eye, I emoted,
was losing its soul.

When I finally did visit the new headquarters, I was
ready to find fault with it. My bias aside, the building did
have one important disadvantage. The site was served by
no public transportation. The bus line on Whippany Road
had been a convenience for visitors and employees as well
as a valuable teaching tool for dogs and students. Another
drawback was that the bedrooms were too small to contain
a desk for a typewriter so that letters had to be written
amid the distraction of the recreation room. In general,
however, the new school functioned well. Yet within a year
of the move, The Seeing Eye lost three members of its
instructing staff to Guiding Eyes for the Blind. The two
events were not unrelated.

Geoffrey Lock left in December 1965 to become Guiding Eyes' chief instructor. William McCracken followed in February 1966. Theodore Zubrycki joined them in September.

Guiding Eyes was guilty of questionable conduct in raiding the staff of a rival school, but The Seeing Eye ought never to have been vulnerable to such a raid. While it had spent a million dollars on its new building, it had remained tightfisted in the matter of salaries. Its Achilles' heel was of its own making. In 1954, George Werntz had seen the school's wealth as so embarrassing a problem that, five years later, the school stopped raising money and began to give it away instead. Yet during this same five-year period, the average annual salary of an instructor rose from $4,164 to $4,716, for an average annual increase of only $110.40, a fraction more than 2 percent.

In fairness to George Werntz, it must be stressed that the school's policy on salaries had been set under Willi Ebeling, who seemed to feel that working for The Seeing Eye required material sacrifice, rather like taking a vow of poverty on joining a religious order. Low salaries were the rule in all departments, including the position of chief executive.

George Werntz did a good deal to improve working conditions and fringe benefits. Instructors were given medical insurance, a pension plan, and a small life insurance policy with premiums paid by the school. Hours were much shorter than in the thirties. Instructors now worked a five-day week. After the first week of class, they rotated night duty, so that one man could go home. George Werntz arranged a lecture series to raise the instructing staff's "level of cultural awareness," but lectures put no meat on the table.

On October 1, 1965, The Seeing Eye's assets had reached an all-time high of $17 million. In the previous fiscal year, the grants program gave away $93,000, enough to more than double the salaries of the entire staff of instructors. Charity, it seemed to them, should begin at home. Geoffrey Lock had taught in England and in San Rafael before coming to The Seeing Eye, yet he was making only $6,400 a year, part of which was a housing allowance.

The annual report that described the defection to Guiding Eyes revealed some soul-searching: "A moderately good man who becomes dissatisfied for any reason possesses a marketable skill in a field in which proliferation is not in the public interest. We have vast resources from which to pay salaries that would soon become so high as to be inconsistent with the type of organization we conceive this to be. To attempt to meet salary offers of pirating organizations is to surrender to a kind of extortion that could result in administrative chaos." Even so, the school adopted a new salary schedule for the instructing staff that provided healthy increases of between 16 and 25 percent. "The median salary being paid mobility instructors, most with a master's degree, is $7,440. The median Seeing Eye instructor will receive $7,950 in the new fiscal year."

With a better paid "faculty" and a new plant, production began to climb. In 1952, when the school had graduated a record 187 students for the second year in a row, the long-sought goal of 200 dogs a year had seemed within grasp, but production had fallen off sharply and sunk to 148 in 1956. Generally speaking, the demand for replacements held steady or increased, but The Seeing Eye was not attracting enough new students. For thirteen consecutive years, replacements outnumbered first-timers, frequently by a wide margin. A number of new students were lost to the rival schools. Others were discouraged by hostile counselors who used *The Demand for Dog Guides* to prove that guide dogs were a passing fad.

The pattern changed in 1967. The new building had won favorable publicity, but the overriding factor was a three-part television series on The Seeing Eye, "Atta Girl, Kelly." It was a Walt Disney production, and George Werntz was responsible for interesting the Disney studio in the project. He worked through Jules Stein, a friend of Disney's who had approached the school for a grant for Research to Prevent Blindness. Following "Atta Girl, Kelly," there was an avalanche of inquiries from potential applicants. In 1967, new students outnumbered replacements for the first time in fourteen years, and in 1968, the school accepted 200 applicants for the first time in history.

Thanks to Disney, applicants were beating a path to The Seeing Eye's door. Thanks to the breeding program, they found an improved quality of dog waiting for them, but quantity was still a problem. The program had started slowly and suffered a number of setbacks. In 1950, for example, it was discovered that an imported brood bitch of excellent temperament had transmitted car sickness to all her progeny. Two years later, epidemics of distemper and hepatitis carried off nineteen puppies. In the beginning, only about 70 percent of the breeding stock sent into training were successful. In 1954, the figure reached 90 percent for the first time. It tended to fluctuate around that figure thereafter, but a physical weakness began to reduce the number of dogs who could be sent into training.

For some time an unrecognized congenital defect had been plaguing dogs of the larger breeds across the country. They developed a weakness in their hips that was particularly undesirable for guide dogs whose forward thrust is generated by their hind legs. What made this hip dysplasia insidious was that it frequently failed to manifest itself until dogs were two or three years old, or even older. In 1955, after it was discovered that dysplasia could be diagnosed by X ray, The Seeing Eye X-rayed all its puppies. For one three-year period, one in every four puppies bred was disqualified for unsound hips.

Diagnosis was valuable, but the cure could be found only through breeding. The male gene proved to be dominant, which meant the analysis could be confined to studs, but even then the problem was tricky. For example, two brothers named Tom and Jerry might have been expected to transmit the same genetic traits, but nearly half of Tom's seventeen pups had dysplasia, while all of Jerry's thirty-three offspring had sound hips.

As the breeding program sought to refine the puppies' heredity, the 4-H program worked to improve their social environment. By 1949, it had so expanded that Robert Curtis was hired to supervise it, and his became a full-time job. In 1950, there were 150 dogs boarding in 4-H homes in ten countics. Many of the dogs came not from Seeing Eye stock, but as gifts from friends of the school. Without the 4-H, The Seeing Eye could not have raised these puppies and would have been forced to refuse many desirable animals.

Bob Curtis visited each home four times a year to examine the puppies and discuss their progress with their families. In most instances, when a dog was mature enough to go into training, Bob replaced it immediately with a new puppy to ease the pain of parting with the old. Families with several children were capable of handling more than one puppy at a time, and these might raise ten, fifteen, or even twenty dogs. Miss Evelyn Henderson, who adopted her first puppy in 1951, later devoted herself to raising fifteen foster children. She has had as many as twelve pups at one time. In the spring of 1978, she received The Seeing Eye's Buddy Award for the incredible feat of having raised more than 200 puppies.

The Seeing Eye encouraged 4-H families to expose their dogs to a variety of experiences, to take them for rides in the car or, if possible, on a bus or train, to walk them on crowded streets, past noisy construction, into shops or supermarkets, anywhere they might be likely to accompany a blind master. The one thing forbidden was to make them walk at heel. They were intended to guide, pulling ahead, not following behind. They must be allowed to tug to their heart's content, and a straining adolescent of ten or twelve months could be hard to hold. But the trouble 4-H boys and girls took with their dogs was well worth it. They proved far superior to kennel-raised dogs when they went into training.

The student population was changing. It was older. It included more women and more diabetics. Students coming back for their third or fourth dog could no longer handle one as strong or as sharp as their first. Women, especially those who had never had a dog before, needed guides that did not pull too hard. The same was true for diabetics. The program tried to breed smaller, gentler, and softer shepherds, but often Labradors and golden retrievers were preferable for the women. The inability to procure enough of them might keep a first-time woman applicant on the waiting list for a year or more.

According to a schedule inagurated in 1955, bitches worthy of breeding were put on the farm at age fifteen months to whelp one or two litters. Then they were spayed and sent into training. They proved to have exceptionally fine temperaments. Motherhood seemed to mature and settle them. Their patience and friendliness were increasingly desirable as urbanization exposed dogs more and more to crowds, confusion, and confinement in cramped spaces. My Hessa had two litters before she went into training, and the patience with which she arranges herself under the seat for an hour-and-a-half bus ride to New York is marvelous. My second dog, Wick, a tall, rangy male who grew to a weight of 110 pounds, could never have gotten into such a small space, and if he had, he would have resented any fellow passengers who crowded him.

Production of both dogs and students picked up markedly after the school moved into the new building. In 1964, when the impact of hip dysplasia was at its worst, only 26 dogs from the breeding program were sent into training. In 1966, the first year at Washington Valley, nearly three times that many graduated with students. The previous high for graduates in a year had been 187. From 1967 to 1972, the average number of graduates was 188. The average number of Seeing Eye-bred dogs paired with them

was 94, just half of the total. New students exceeded replacements every year, and the percentages of women graduates climbed. In 1972, the school fell just short of 200
graduates with 198, of which 88 or 44 percent were women.
But just at this point, there was renewed discontent in the
instructing staff and a serious setback in the breeding
program.

Inflation was eroding the value of the dollar. The area
around Morristown had attracted many high-income families, and the demand for housing sent real estate prices
soaring. It was impossible to live anywhere nearby on an
instructor's salary, and driving many miles to and from
work made the instructors feel like second-class citizens,
commuting from low-income ghettos.

Another irritant was the awareness of the expanding
grants program. Between 1958 and 1968, The Seeing Eye
had given away more than $2 million. After January 1967,
when an executive was employed to administer it full-time,
the grants program accelerated. For the five-year period up
to and including 1972, the average of annual grants awarded
was a shade over $900,000. Yet despite this largesse, the
market value of Seeing Eye securities of October 1, 1972,
exceeded $29 million. The trustees could hardly cry poverty.

Torn between loyalty to the school and desperation
with inflation, the staff of instructors petitioned the board
to make a comprehensive review of their salary structure.
George Werntz and the trustees took their petition seriously.
Personnel officers of Merck and Co. and the Bank of New
York were engaged to study the situation. They recommended a new salary schedule calling for increases of from
14 to 22.5 percent, which the board formally adopted in
May 1973. The new annual salaries ranged from $8,400 for
a beginning apprentice to $25,000 for the director. As
George Werntz commented, instructors' salaries were at last
competitive with those of other educational institutions in
the area. Faculty morale soared.

It was high time to deal with the breeding program.

The record high of 120 Mendham-bred dogs in 1970 had fallen off in successive years to 100, then to 81, finally to 74. The size of the average litter was so small that even lower production might be expected in future. In this emergency, Debby Debetaz was called back from his retirement and put in charge of the Mendham farm.

His analysis pointed to a variety of defects. The breeding stock was too limited and too closely related. Of the twenty-four bitches and four studs, only two bitches came from outside bloodlines. Both bitches and studs were overage, and the bitches had been bred too frequently, some every time they came in season. These factors, plus linebreeding and inbreeding, had led to small litters and unhealthy puppies. The strain of producing the bumper crops of 1969 and 1970 had exhausted the stock, which ought to have been renewed from outside sources. To put it in oversimplified terms, The Seeing Eye had been putting too much money into grants and not enough into dogs.

Even with an adequate supply of money, good breeding stock was hard to find. Some of the most desirable dogs were not for sale. Many of those with good temperament were dysplastic. On a trip to Switzerland and France, Debby found that all the dogs with sound hips were too big or too sharp. While the school looked for suitable new dogs, overaged animals were retired from the program. A new breeding schedule permitted brood bitches to rest for one season in every three. Plans for expanded and up-to-date new breeding kennels were under way. A thorough overhauling of the breeding program had been instituted by the time George Werntz retired on August 1, 1975.

He was succeeded by Stuart Grout, who had been Director of Academic Planning at Boston University and who had had broad experience in many aspects of university administration both there and at the University of Arkansas. He had been awarded a Ph.D. in educational administration from the University of Chicago in 1956, but Stuart was not the sort who styled himself Dr. Grout. He reported to work on May 1, and like George Werntz, trained two dogs for a class of two students. Otherwise, his was a short apprenticeship.

Many programs launched under George were continued or accelerated by Stuart. The grants program has been cut back radically. Its director has been let go, and it has been renamed the support program. Before he retired, George had the satisfaction of achieving the goal of 200 graduates in 1974—201, to be exact—but Stuart has seen totals of 204, 217, and in this, the school's fiftieth year, 214. It seems likely that *The Demand for Dog Guides* underestimated the number of blind people who could be motivated to use guide dogs, once the new breed of smaller, and softer dogs had brought guide work within their physical capability. The Seeing Eye expects to operate at peak capacity of more than 200 graduates annually for an indefinite period.

The breeding farm has just added enlarged modern kennels. A new man, Robert Wichman, has been put in charge of a revitalized program. He has not only added new shepherd stock, some of it imported from Germany, but has begun a program for breeding Labradors as well. The 4-H is now nearing a target of 300 dogs boarding with families.

In George Werntz's last year, the instructing staff added women apprentices after a lapse of more than forty years since the days of Adelaide Clifford and Missy Doudge. Currently there are three, Kathie Waite, Kathy Winkleman, and Sharon Griswold, with a new apprentice, Patricia Rogers. Dick Krokus is the director of a staff of twelve in all, and although physical wear and tear has forced one man to retire with a heart condition and another to take a different job at the school because of a bad back, morale is high.

The pressures of inflation have at last caught up with the school's investment income. In order to keep abreast of rising costs, the Board of Trustees has revived a low-key membership enrollment directed at former Seeing Eye supporters and friends. A deferred giving program is also being developed in connection with long range planning. At the same time, Jobson Associates continues its educational efforts with its film library, *The Guide,* and multiple contacts with the media.

Paula Purseley has been heading the division for student services ever since Elizabeth Hutchinson retired in 1965, and of course, there have been many other personnel changes. People will come, and people will go, but there will always be dogs, and today dogs are back where they belong—at the center of The Seeing Eye's program.

Cooperation between The Seeing Eye and the other leading guide-dog schools is greater today than at any time in the past. Guiding Eyes has become a first-rate school. I must here emphatically insist that, while I have reported some questionable behavior in Guiding Eyes' past, this does not at all reflect on its present program. Representatives of The Seeing Eye and Guiding Eyes have exchanged on-site visits, and Stuart Grout expresses sincere admiration for The Seeing Eye's former *bête noir.*

In the summer of 1978, the leadership of the four big schools, Guide Dogs for the Blind, Guiding Eyes, Leader, and The Seeing Eye, met for the first time to exchange ideas and information. There are still differences of opinion, but the rivalry is friendly. Between them, they graduated fewer than 450 students fifteen years ago. Their combined output will approach 800 this year, and all have long lists of applicants waiting. Their future cooperation will help to ensure that each is making a better mousetrap.

Conclusion

As I DRAW this book to a close, I see I have written less a history than a paean, a panegyric to the vision of Dorothy Eustis, the genius of Jack Humphrey, the courage of Morris Frank, the faith of Willi Ebeling, and the selflessness and hard work of all four. Nor by singling out these four do I mean in any way to discount the contributions of Debby Debetaz, Marian Jobson, Mary Dranga Campbell, Ibby Hutchinson, Gretchen Green, and literally dozens more I could name.

The overwhelming characteristic of The Seeing Eye to me is its utter selflessness, but a selflessness that is combined with keen intellect, scientific method, iron self-discipline, and hard work. In the fall of 1957, I roomed with a diabetic who had been a bricklayer in Chicago. He had had little formal education, and he invariably said "youse" instead of "you," but he had as much courage as any man I have ever met.

His diabetes was far advanced. His circulation was so poor that the exertion of walking affected his extremities after a short time, and he fell frequently. When I would ask how a trip had gone, he would answer cheerfully, "Me and Spot only fell down tree times dis trip."

One of the other students, who apparently knew a good deal about diabetes, confided to me that my roommate could not have more than six months to live. I am as certain as I can be that George Werntz and Ibby Hutchinson and the other members of the top staff knew his medical history and his prognosis. But people who have seen the continuing miracle of guide dogs year after year learn to believe in miracles. This man wanted a dog. He had the guts to train with a dog. He must be given the chance. Against all the odds, The Seeing Eye gave. And my roommate gave. And his dog Spot gave. And he went back to Chicago with a dog. What happened then was not quite a miracle. He was not cured of diabetes, but he lived another three and a half years with the independence and dignity Spot gave him.

I believe I understood Uncle Willi's failings, but I retain an abiding admiration for him. What made Uncle Willi great was his constantly renewing awareness of the miracle of the dogs.

I recall a visit to the old headquarters shortly before Uncle Willi was to retire. Although he was at least seventy and had been at the school nearly a quarter of a century, he was in high excitement about an incident that had taken place the day before. A dog that had been with his new master three days had misbehaved at lunch, and when the instructor went to correct it, it growled at him. My wife and I did not understand, and Uncle Willi had to explain.

"After only three days, mind you, the dog takes over the new master." In a voice vibrant with delight, he repeated, "Only three days. And when the instructor comes to give a correction, he growls. He says, 'This is my guy here. If there is any correcting, he does it. Not you.'"

Ned Myrose told me of his experience with what may possibly have been the same dog. He assigned a Dalmatian named Nosey to a marine veteran.

"Three days after I gave him the dog, I couldn't get near him. Nosey would come at my throat, and he meant business." That was not all. "Every time they stopped for a down curb, Nosey would lift his leg and wet on him. Good thing he was a marine instead of an old lady. He thought it was funny."

As soon as they left the school, both Nosey's aggressiveness and the wetting ceased. The probable explanation is that Nosey had had an uncertain youth, shunted from one owner to another. When he was paired with the marine, Nosey had found the master he wanted and turned on Myrose in the fear that he was trying to take him away. Once in his master's home, he had no more fear and showed no more hostility.

The wetting had a similar cause. Urinating is the way a dog claims possession. He was telling his master, "I own you." At home, when he no longer feared separation, he had no need to assert possession. In a curious way, then, both the aggression and the urination had been Nosey's way of expressing love.

In the course of fifty years, some variation of this miracle of love has been repeated nearly 7,500 times. Blind men and women of all ages have come from all parts of the United States and Canada, from many different walks of life and many different national origins. Some have had poor orientation. Others were frail from lack of exercise. But if they had the faith to trust their dogs and the capacity to win their dogs' love, even the most unlikely went away confident in their ability to lead a new life. Perhaps no one said it better than Larry Liggin:

> The dog is my shepherd, just what I want. She maketh me to rise early every morning. She leadeth me beside garbage cans and parking meters, and she restoreth my freedom. She guideth me in the paths of safety for my life's sake. Yea, though I walk through the thunder of the railroad station and among the mongrels of Flagler Street, I will fear no evil, for she is with me. The creak of her harness and the jingle of her collar, they comfort me. She prepareth a way before me in the presence of all confusion. She cov-

ereth my hand with affectionate licks and nibbles, and my love for her runneth over. Surely, with affection and correction, I shall follow her all the days of her life, and she will dwell in my heart forever.

Index

Index

sheltered workshops, 24, 25, 104, 108, 123
Shepherd Dog Review, 5, 59, 67
Sinclair, Mervyn, 24–25, 97, 99, 100–101, 102, 110, 115, 123, 124, 130, 131, 132, 135–136, 142, 154
Strong, Harold, 139–140, 145
Synikin, John L., 14–15, 74, 109, 175

Tarkington, Booth, 144, 157–158, 161
trainers, *see* instructors

Van Cleve, Edward, 23, 69, 75

Weagley, John, 196
Weber, Josef, 15, 59, 60, 62, 63, 65–66, 67, 76–84, 102, 175
Werntz, George, Jr., 155, 195, 196–205, 210, 215, 216, 217, 220
Whitstock, Robert, 200–202
Wigger von Blaisienberg, 10–11
Wood, Dorothy Harrison, *see* Eustis
Wood, Harrison, 3, 19, 128, 194–195
Wood, Walter A. III, 3, 4, 19, 31, 43, 45
Woollcott, Alexander, 6, 51, 142–143, 144
Working Dogs, 10, 89, 90
working dogs, *see also* guide dogs, 3, 8, 10, 28–29, 46, 47